Draw a Picture of You and Your Dad

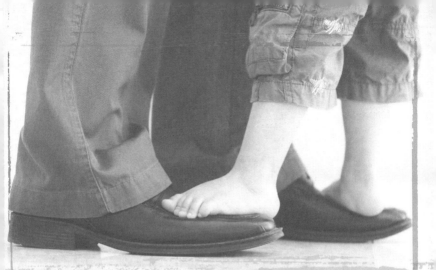

Daddy & Me

100 Daily Devos
for Dads and Their Little Boys

The quoted ideas expressed in this book (but not Scripture verses) are not, in all cases, exact quotations, as some have been edited for clarity and brevity. In all cases, the author has attempted to maintain the speaker's original intent. In some cases, quoted material for this book was obtained from secondary sources, primarily print media. While every effort was made to ensure the accuracy of these sources, the accuracy cannot be guaranteed. For additions, deletions, corrections, or clarifications in future editions of this text, please write Freeman-Smith.

Scripture quotations are taken from:

The Holy Bible, King James Version (KJV)

The Holy Bible, New International Version (NIV) Copyright © 1973, 1978, 1984, by International Bible Society. Used by permission of Zondervan Publishing House. All rights reserved.

The Holy Bible, New King James Version (NKJV) Copyright © 1982 by Thomas Nelson, Inc. Used by permission.

Holy Bible, New Living Translation, (NLT) copyright © 1996. Used by permission of Tyndale House Publishers, Inc., Wheaton, Illinois 60189. All rights reserved.

The Message (MSG)- This edition issued by contractual arrangement with NavPress, a division of The Navigators, U.S.A. Originally published by NavPress in English as THE MESSAGE: The Bible in Contemporary Language copyright 2002-2003 by Eugene Peterson. All rights reserved.

New Century Version®. (NCV) Copyright © 1987, 1988, 1991 by Word Publishing, a division of Thomas Nelson, Inc. All rights reserved. Used by permission.

The New American Standard Bible®, (NASB) Copyright © 1960, 1962, 1963, 1968, 1971, 1972, 1973, 1975, 1977, 1995 by The Lockman Foundation. Used by permission.

International Children's Bible®, New Century Version®. (ICB) Copyright © 1986, 1988, 1999 by Tommy Nelson™, a division of Thomas Nelson, Inc. All rights reserved. Used by permission.

The Holy Bible, The Living Bible (TLB), Copyright © 1971 owned by assignment by Illinois Regional Bank N.A. (as trustee). Used by permission of Tyndale House Publishers, Inc., Wheaton, Illinois 60189. All rights reserved.

The Holman Christian Standard Bible™ (HCSB) Copyright © 1999, 2000, 2001 by Holman Bible Publishers. Used by permission.

Cover Design by Kim Russell / Wahoo Designs
Page Layout by Bart Dawson

ISBN 978-1-60587-361-9

Printed in the United States of America

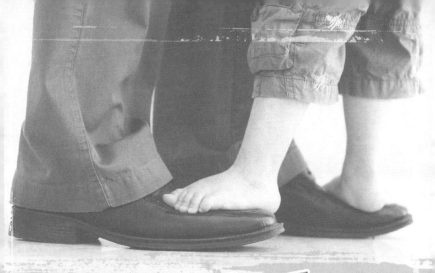

Daddy & Me

100 Daily Devos
for Dads and Their Little Boys

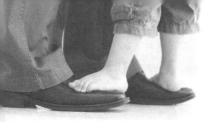

A Message to Dads

Perhaps your son's library is already overflowing with brightly colored children's books. If so, congratulations: you're a thoughtful father who understands the importance of reading to your youngster. This little book is an important addition to your child's library. It is intended to be read by Christian dads to their young sons.

For the next 100 days, try this experiment: read one chapter each night to your son, and then spend a few more moments talking about the chapter's meaning. When you do, you will have 100 different opportunities to share God's wisdom with your boy, and that's a very good thing.

If you have been touched by God's love and His grace, then you know the joy that He has brought into your own life. Now it's your turn to share His message with the boy whom He has entrusted to your care. Happy reading! And may God richly bless you and your family now and forever.

Jesus Gives Life

Then Jesus said, "I am the bread that gives life. Whoever comes to me will never be hungry, and whoever believes in me will never be thirsty."

John 6:35 NCV

Who's the best friend any boy has ever had? And who's the best friend the whole world has ever had? Jesus, of course! When you invite Him into your heart, Jesus will be your friend, too . . . your friend forever.

Jesus has offered to share the gifts of everlasting life and everlasting love with the world . . . and with you. If you make mistakes, He'll still be your friend. If you behave badly, He'll still love you. If you feel sorry or sad, He can help you feel better.

Jesus wants you to have a happy, healthy life. He wants you to be generous and kind. He wants you to follow His example. And the rest is up to you. You can do it! And with a friend like Jesus, you will.

A Timely Tip for Boys

Jesus is your true friend. He loves you, and He offers you eternal life with Him in heaven. Welcome Him into your heart. Now!

More from God's Word

I have come as a light into the world, so that everyone who believes in Me would not remain in darkness.

John 12:46 HCSB

We have seen it and we testify and declare to you the eternal life that was with the Father and was revealed to us—what we have seen and heard we also declare to you, so that you may have fellowship along with us; and indeed our fellowship is with the Father and with His Son Jesus Christ.

1 John 1:2-4 HCSB

Jesus Christ is the same yesterday, today, and forever.

Hebrews 13:8 HCSB

A Timely Tip for Dads

Jesus is the light of the world. As a caring dad, it's up to you to make certain that He's the light of your family, too.

Some Very Bright Ideas

Jesus is not a strong man making men and women who gather around Him weak. He is the Strong creating the strong.

E. Stanley Jones

Jesus was the perfect reflection of God's nature in every situation He encountered during His time here on earth.

Bill Hybels

Jesus is the light of the world. God wants Him to be the light of your life.

Criswell Freeman

A Father-Son Prayer

Dear Lord, we know that Jesus loves us. Please let us share His love with others so that through us people can understand what it means to follow Christ. Amen

Devo 2

Starting Your Day with God

It is good to give thanks to the Lord, to sing praises to the Most High. It is good to proclaim your unfailing love in the morning, your faithfulness in the evening.

Psalm 92:1-2 NLT

How do you start your day? Do you sleep until the last possible moment and then hop out of bed without giving a single thought to God? Hopefully not. If you're smart, you'll start your day with a prayer of thanks to your Heavenly Father.

Each new day is a gift from God, and if you're wise, you'll spend a few quiet moments thanking the Giver. It's a wonderful way to start your day.

A Timely Tip for Boys

Make an appointment with God every day, and keep it. Reading your Bible and saying your prayers are important things to do. Very important. So please don't forget to talk with God every day.

More from God's Word

Morning by morning he wakens me and opens my understanding to his will. The Sovereign Lord has spoken to me, and I have listened.

Isaiah 50:4-5 NLT

Be still, and know that I am God.

Psalm 46:10 NKJV

But grow in the grace and knowledge of our Lord and Savior Jesus Christ. To Him be the glory both now and to the day of eternity.

2 Peter 3:18 HCSB

A Timely Tip for Dads

Daily devotionals never go out of style. Are you too busy to lead a daily devotional with your family? If so, it's time to reorder your priorities.

Some Very Bright Ideas

Morning praise will make your days.

Anonymous

Meditating upon His Word will inevitably bring peace of mind, strength of purpose, and power for living.

Bill Bright

A child of God should never leave his bedroom in the morning without being on good terms with God.

C. H. Spurgeon

A Father-Son Prayer

Dear Lord, the Bible teaches us that we should turn to You often, and that's what we will do today and every day. Amen

Devo 3

Setting an Example

Set an example of good works yourself, with integrity and dignity in your teaching.

Titus 2:7 HCSB

The Bible says that you are "the light that gives light to the world." The Bible also says that you should live in a way that lets other people understand what it means to be a good person. And of course, learning to share is an important part of being a good person.

What kind of "light" have you been giving off? Hopefully, you have been a good example for everybody to see. Why? Because the world needs all the light it can get, and that includes your light, too!

A Timely Tip for Boys

Think about the ways that your behavior impacts your family and friends.

More from God's Word

For the kingdom of God is not in talk but in power.

1 Corinthians 4:20 HCSB

Therefore since we also have such a large cloud of witnesses surrounding us, let us lay aside every weight and the sin that so easily ensnares us, and run with endurance the race that lies before us.

Hebrews 12:1 HCSB

Test all things; hold fast what is good. Abstain from every form of evil.

1 Thessalonians 5:21-22 NKJV

A Timely Tip for Dads

Make your actions consistent with your words. Parental pronouncements are easy to make but much harder to live by. But whether you like it or not, you are almost certainly the most important role model for your child. Behave accordingly.

Some Very Bright Ideas

It's good to be saved and know it! It's also good to be saved and show it!

Anonymous

Are you willing to follow the light—are you willing to be the light?

Criswell Freeman

More depends on my walk than my talk.

D. L. Moody

A Father-Son Prayer

Dear Lord, let our lights shine brightly for You. Let us be positive examples for all to see, and let us share love and kindness with our family and friends. Amen

Feeling Better

A wise person is patient. He will be honored if he ignores a wrong done against him.

Proverbs 19:11 ICB

Is forgiving someone else an easy thing for you to do or a hard thing? If you're like most people, forgiving others can be hard, Hard, HARD! But even if you're having a very hard time forgiving someone, you can do it if you talk things over with your parents, and if you talk things over with God.

Do you find forgiveness difficult? Talk about it and pray about it. You'll feel better when you do.

A Timely Tip for Boys

Forgive . . . and keep forgiving! Sometimes, you may forgive someone once and then, at a later time, become angry at the very same person again. If so, you must forgive that person again and again . . . until it sticks!

More from God's Word

Praise the Lord, I tell myself, and never forget the good things he does for me. He forgives all my sins and heals all my diseases.
Psalm 103:3 NLT

Therefore, if you are offering your gift at the altar and there remember that your brother has something against you, leave your gift there in front of the altar. First go and be reconciled to your brother, then come and offer your gift.
Matthew 5:23-24 NIV

And be ye kind one to another, tenderhearted, forgiving one another, even as God for Christ's sake hath forgiven you.
Ephesians 4:32 KJV

A Timely Tip for Dads

If you want your son to learn the art of forgiveness, then you must master that art yourself. If you're able to forgive those who have hurt you and, by doing so, move on with your life, your kids will learn firsthand that forgiveness is God's way.

Some Very Bright Ideas

When God forgives, He forgets. He buries our sins in the sea and puts a sign on the shore saying, "No Fishing Allowed."

Corrie ten Boom

The work of forgiveness begins with prayer.

Criswell Freeman

Every time we forgive others, deserving it or not, we have a reminder of God's forgiveness.

Franklin Graham

God forgets the past. Imitate him.

Max Lucado

A Father-Son Prayer

Dear Lord, even when forgiveness is hard, help us be people who forgive others, just as You have forgiven us. Amen

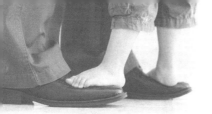

Solomon Says . . . Be Kind!

A kind person is doing himself a favor. But a cruel person brings trouble upon himself.

Proverbs 11:17 ICB

King Solomon wrote most of the Book of Proverbs; in it, he gave us wonderful advice for living wisely. Solomon warned that unkind behavior leads only to trouble, but kindness is its own reward.

The next time you're tempted to say an unkind word, remember Solomon. He was one of the wisest men who ever lived, and he knew that it's always better to be kind. And now, you know it, too.

A Timely Tip for Boys

Kindness should be part of our lives every day, not just on the days when we feel good. Don't try to be kind some of the time, and don't try to be kind to some of the people you know. Instead, try to be kind all of the time, and try to be kind to all the people you know. Remember, the Golden Rule starts with you!

More from God's Word

A kind man benefits himself, but a cruel man brings disaster on himself.

Proverbs 11:17 HCSB

Love is patient; love is kind.

1 Corinthians 13:4 HCSB

Therefore, God's chosen ones, holy and loved, put on heartfelt compassion, kindness, humility, gentleness, and patience.

Colossians 3:12 HCSB

A Timely Tip for Dads

Your son will learn how to treat others by watching you (not by listening to you!). Acts of kindness speak louder than words.

Some Very Bright Ideas

One of the greatest things a man can do for his heavenly Father is to be kind to some of his other children.

Henry Drummond

When you launch an act of kindness out into the crosswinds of life, it will blow kindness back to you.

Dennis Swanberg

Showing kindness to others is one of the nicest things we can do for ourselves.

Janette Oke

A Father-Son Prayer

Dear Lord, sometimes it's easy to be nice to people and sometimes it's not so easy. When it's hard to be kind, Lord, help us say the right things and do the right things. Amen

Draw a Picture Together about Being Kind

Devo 6

Love to Share

And we have known and believed the love that God has for us. God is love, and he who abides in love abides in God, and God in him.

1 John 4:16 NKJV

The Bible tells us that God is love and that if we wish to know Him, we must have love in our hearts. Sometimes, of course, when we're tired, angry, or frustrated, it is very hard for us to be loving. Thankfully, anger and frustration are feelings that come and go, but God's love lasts forever.

If you'd like to improve your day and your life, share God's love with your family and friends. Every time you love, and every time you give, God smiles.

A Timely Tip for Boys

God's love is our greatest security blanket: Kay Arthur advises, "Snuggle in God's arms. When you are hurting, when you feel lonely or left out, let Him cradle you, comfort you, reassure you of His all-sufficient power and love." Enough said.

More from God's Word

Help me, Lord my God; save me according to Your faithful love.
Psalm 109:26 HCSB

Whoever is wise will observe these things, and they will understand the lovingkindness of the Lord.
Psalm 107:43 NKJV

The Lord is gracious and compassionate, slow to anger and great in faithful love. The Lord is good to everyone; His compassion [rests] on all He has made.
Psalm 145:8-9 HCSB

A Timely Tip for Dads

You know that "God is love." Now, it's your responsibility to make certain that your children know it, too.

Some Very Bright Ideas

God will never let you be shaken or moved from your place near His heart.

Joni Eareckson Tada

To be loved by God is the highest relationship, the highest achievement, and the highest position of life.

Henry Blackaby and Claude King

God has pursued us from farther than space and longer than time.

John Eldredge

A Father-Son Prayer

Dear Lord, the Bible teaches us that You are love. And, we know that You love us. We will accept Your love—and share it—now and always. Amen

Choosing Wisely

I am offering you life or death, blessings or curses. Now, choose life! . . . To choose life is to love the Lord your God, obey him, and stay close to him.

Deuteronomy 30:19-20 NCV

Choices, choices, choices! You've got so many choices to make, and sometimes making those choices isn't easy. At times, you're torn between what you want to do and what you ought to do. When that happens, it's up to you to choose wisely.

When you make wise choices, you are rewarded; when you make unwise choices, you must accept the consequences. It's as simple as that. So make sure that your choices are pleasing to God . . . or else!

A Timely Tip for Boys

Wise choices bring you happiness; unwise choices don't. So whenever you have a choice to make, choose wisely.

More from God's Word

People with integrity have firm footing, but those who follow crooked paths will slip and fall.

Proverbs 10:9 NLT

Now it happened as they went that He entered a certain village; and a certain woman named Martha welcomed Him into her house. And she had a sister called Mary, who also sat at Jesus' feet and heard His word. But Martha was distracted with much serving, and she approached Him and said, "Lord, do You not care that my sister has left me to serve alone? Therefore tell her to help me." And Jesus answered and said to her, "Martha, Martha, you are worried and troubled about many things. But one thing is needed, and Mary has chosen that good part, which will not be taken away from her."

Luke 10:38-42 NKJV

A Timely Tip for Dads

Of course you want to give your children room to grow, but some decisions must be reserved for the wisest, most mature men and women of the family (moms and dads). Big decisions, especially decisions about health and safety, should be made by thoughtful parents, not children.

Some Very Bright Ideas

Life is pretty much like a cafeteria line—it offers us many choices, both good and bad. The Christian must have a spiritual radar that detects the difference not only between bad and good but also among good, better, and best.

Dennis Swanberg

God expresses His love in giving us the freedom to choose.

Charles Stanley

I do not know how the Spirit of Christ performs it, but He brings us choices through which we constantly change, fresh and new, into His likeness.

Joni Eareckson Tada

A Father-Son Prayer

Dear God, we have many choices to make. Help us choose wisely as we follow in the footsteps of Your Son. Amen

Devo 8

Your Attitude

Make your own attitude that of Christ Jesus.

Philippians 2:5 HCSB

What's an attitude? The word "attitude" means "the way that you think." And don't forget this: your attitude is important.

Your attitude can make you happy or sad, grumpy or glad, joyful or mad. And, your attitude doesn't just control the way that you think; it also controls how you behave. If you have a good attitude, you'll behave well. And if you have a bad attitude, you're more likely to misbehave.

Have you spent any time thinking about the way that you think? Do you pay much attention to your attitude? Hopefully so! After all, a good attitude is better than a bad one . . . lots better.

You have more control over your attitude than you think. So do your best to make your attitude a good attitude. One way you can do that is by learning about Jesus and about His attitude toward life. When you do, you'll learn that it's always better to think good thoughts, and it's always better to do good things. Always!

A Timely Tip for Boys

What will you pay attention to tomorrow? Try to pay careful attention to God's blessings, to God's love, and to God's rules. When you do, you'll be happier.

More from God's Word

Finally brothers, whatever is true, whatever is honorable, whatever is just, whatever is pure, whatever is lovely, whatever is commendable—if there is any moral excellence and if there is any praise—dwell on these things.

Philippians 4:8 HCSB

Set your minds on what is above, not on what is on the earth.

Colossians 3:2 HCSB

A Timely Tip for Dads

Parental attitudes are contagious. It's up to you to live your life—and treat your family—in a way that pleases God because He's watching carefully . . . and so, for that matter, are your kids.

Some Very Bright Ideas

Life goes on. Keep on smiling and the whole world smiles with you.

Dennis Swanberg

It never hurts your eyesight to look on the bright side of things.

Barbara Johnson

Attitude is more important than the past, than education, than money, than circumstances, than what people do or say. It is more important than appearance, giftedness, or skill.

Charles Swindoll

A Father-Son Prayer

Dear Lord, help us have an attitude that is pleasing to You. And, let us remember to count our blessings today, tomorrow, and every day after that. Amen

No Secrets

The eyes of the Lord are in every place, keeping watch . . . .

Proverbs 15:3 NKJV

Even when nobody else is watching, God is. Nothing that we say or do escapes the watchful eye of our Lord. God understands that we are not perfect, but He also wants us to live according to His rules, not our own.

The next time that you're tempted to say something that you shouldn't say or to do something that you shouldn't do, remember that you can't keep secrets from God. So don't even try!

A Timely Tip for Boys

Having trouble hearing God? If so, slow yourself down, tune out the distractions, and listen carefully. God has important things to say; your task is to be still and listen.

More from God's Word

The Lord is near all who call out to Him, all who call out to Him with integrity. He fulfills the desires of those who fear Him; He hears their cry for help and saves them.

Psalm 145:18-19 HCSB

I am not alone, because the Father is with Me.

John 16:32 HCSB

Fear not, for I am with you; Be not dismayed, for I am your God. I will strengthen you.

Isaiah 41:10 NKJV

A Timely Tip for Dads

Of course you know that God watches over you, but you must also make certain that your children know that you know.

Some Very Bright Ideas

Every secret act of character, conviction, and courage has been observed in living color by our omniscient God.

Bill Hybels

God possesses infinite knowledge and awareness which is uniquely His. At all times, even in the midst of any type of suffering, I can realize that he knows, loves, watches, understands, and more than that, He has a purpose.

Billy Graham

God knows that we, with our limited vision, don't even know that for which we should pray. When we entrust our requests to him, we trust him to honor our prayers with holy judgment.

Max Lucado

A Father-Son Prayer

Dear Lord, we know that You are everywhere and that You are always with us. Today and every day, we will thank You, Father, for Your protection and for Your love. Amen

Think Before You Speak

To everything there is a season...a time to keep silence, and a time to speak.

Ecclesiastes 3:1, 7 KJV

Sometimes, it's easier to say the wrong thing than it is to say the right thing—especially if we're in a hurry to blurt out the first words that come into our heads. But, if we are patient and if we choose our words carefully, we can help other people feel better, and that's exactly what God wants us to do.

The Book of Proverbs tells us that the right words, spoken at the right time, can be wonderful gifts to our families and to our friends. That's why we should think about the things that we say before we say them, not after. When we do, our words make the world a better place, and that's exactly what God wants!

A Timely Tip for Boys

If you can't think of something nice to say . . . don't say anything. Sometimes, the best use of a mouth is to keep it closed.

More from God's Word

Pleasant words are a honeycomb: sweet to the taste and health to the body.

Proverbs 16:24 HCSB

For the one who wants to love life and to see good days must keep his tongue from evil and his lips from speaking deceit.

1 Peter 3:10 HCSB

Avoid irreverent, empty speech, for this will produce an even greater measure of godlessness.

2 Timothy 2:16 HCSB

A Timely Tip for Dads

Words, words, words . . . are important, important, important! And, some of the most important words you will ever speak are the ones that your children hear. So whether or not you are talking directly to your kids, choose your words carefully.

Some Very Bright Ideas

If you can't think of something nice to say, keep thinking.

Criswell Freeman

The great test of a man's character is his tongue.

Oswald Chambers

Attitude and the spirit in which we communicate are as important as the words we say.

Charles Stanley

It is time that the followers of Jesus revise their language and learn to speak respectfully of non-Christian peoples.

Lottie Moon

A Father-Son Prayer

Dear Lord, we know that the words we speak are important. Today, help us think about our words before we say them, not after. Amen

Love That Lasts

It is good and pleasant when God's people live together in peace!

Psalm 133:1 NCV

Are your friends kind to you? And are your friends nice to other people, too? If so, congratulations! If not, it's probably time to start looking for a few new friends. After all, it's really not very much fun to be around people who aren't nice to everybody.

The Bible teaches that a pure heart is a wonderful blessing. It's up to each of us to fill our hearts with love for God, love for Jesus, and love for all people. When we do, we feel better about ourselves.

Do you want to be the best person you can be? Then invite the love of Christ into your heart and share His love with your family and friends. And remember that lasting love always comes from a pure heart . . . like yours!

A Timely Tip for Boys

The best rule for making and keeping friends . . . is the Golden one.

More from God's Word

As iron sharpens iron, a friend sharpens a friend.

Proverbs 27:17 NLT

Beloved, if God so loved us, we also ought to love one another.

1 John 4:11 NKJV

This is my command: Love one another the way I loved you. This is the very best way to love. Put your life on the line for your friends.

John 15:12-13 MSG

A Timely Tip for Dads

If you want your son to choose his friends wisely, you should, too. When you, the parent, choose friends who make you a better person, you'll lead by example.

Some Very Bright Ideas

Insomuch as any one pushes you nearer to God, he or she is your friend.

Anonymous

If you choose to awaken a passion for God, you will have to choose your friends wisely.

Lisa Bevere

A friend who loves will be more concerned about what is best for you than being accepted by you.

Charles Stanley

A Father-Son Prayer

Dear Lord, we thank You for our friends. Please let us be trustworthy friends to other people, and let our friends know how much we love them. Amen

Devo 12

Obeying God

But be doers of the word and not hearers only.

James 1:22 HCSB

How can you show God how much you love Him? By obeying His commandments, that's how! When you follow God's rules, you show Him that you have real respect for Him and for His Son.

Sometimes, you will be tempted to disobey God, but don't do it. And sometimes you'll be tempted to disobey your parents or your teachers . . . but don't do that, either.

When your parent steps away or a teacher looks away, it's up to you to control yourself. And of this you can be sure: If you really want to control yourself, you can do it!

A Timely Tip for Boys

Associate with friends who, by their words and actions, encourage you to obey God.

More from God's Word

Make the most of every opportunity.

Colossians 4:5 NIV

Let us not lose heart in doing good, for in due time we shall reap if we do not grow weary. So then, while we have opportunity, let us do good to all men, and especially to those who are of the household of the faith.

Galatians 6:9-10 NASB

Dear brothers and sisters, whenever trouble comes your way, let it be an opportunity for joy. For when your faith is tested, your endurance has a chance to grow. So let it grow, for when your endurance is fully developed, you will be strong in character and ready for anything.

James 1:2-4 NLT

A Timely Tip for Dads

Being a popular dad isn't nearly as important as being a godly dad. So, when there's a choice between pleasing your kids or pleasing your God, please God.

Some Very Bright Ideas

Joy is the direct result of having God's perspective on our daily lives and the effect of loving our Lord enough to obey His commands and trust His promises.

Bill Bright

When God says, "Go!", it is not a suggestion but a command.

Vance Havner

God uses ordinary people who are obedient to Him to do extraordinary things.

John Maxwell

A Father-Son Prayer

Dear Lord, we want to be obedient Christians. Today and every day, help us understand Your rules and obey them. Amen

Be Thankful

*Our prayers for you are always spilling over into thanksgivings.
We can't quit thanking God our Father and Jesus our Messiah
for you!*

Colossians 1:3 MSG

Are you a thankful boy? You should be! Whether you realize it or not, you have much to be thankful for. And who has given you all the blessings you enjoy? Your parents are responsible, of course. But all of our blessings really start with God.

All of us should make thanksgiving a habit. Since we have been given so much, the least we can do is say "Thank You" to the One who has given us more blessings than we can possibly ever count.

A Timely Tip for Boys

When is the best time to say "thanks" to God? Any time. God loves you all the time, and that's exactly why you should praise Him all the time.

More from God's Word

Oh my soul, bless GOD, don't forget a single blessing!

Psalm 103:2 MSG

O come, let us sing unto the LORD: let us make a joyful noise to the rock of our salvation. Let us come before his presence with thanksgiving, and make a joyful noise unto him with psalms.

Psalm 95:1-2 KJV

I know that the righteous personally thank you, that good people are secure in your presence.

Psalm 140:13 MSG

A Timely Tip for Dads

Of course you are thankful to God for all His blessings, starting with your family. Make certain your children know how you feel.

Some Very Bright Ideas

Don't have anything to be thankful for? Check your pulse!

Anonymous

The joy of the Holy Spirit is experienced by giving thanks in all situations.

Bill Bright

Praise and thank God for who He is and for what He has done for you.

Billy Graham

A Father-Son Prayer

Lord, You have plans for us that are bigger and better than we can imagine. We will trust You to take care of us, and we will try our best to obey Your rules, now and always. Amen

Devo 14

If You're Trying to Be Perfect

The Lord says, "Forget what happened before, and do not think about the past. Look at the new thing I am going to do. It is already happening. Don't you see it? I will make a road in the desert and rivers in the dry land."

Isaiah 43:18-19 NCV

If you're trying to be perfect, you're trying to do something that's impossible. No matter how much you try, you can't be a perfect person . . . and that's okay.

God doesn't expect you to live a mistake-free life—and neither should you. In the game of life, God expects you to try, but He doesn't always expect you to win. Sometimes, you'll make mistakes, but even then, you shouldn't give up!

So remember this: you don't have to be perfect to be a wonderful person. In fact, you don't even need to be "almost-perfect." You simply must try your best and leave the rest up to God.

A Timely Tip for Boys

Don't be too hard on yourself: you don't have to be perfect to be wonderful.

More from God's Word

Those who wait for perfect weather will never plant seeds; those who look at every cloud will never harvest crops. Plant early in the morning, and work until evening, because you don't know if this or that will succeed. They might both do well.

Ecclesiastes 11:4, 6 NCV

Your beliefs about these things should be kept secret between you and God. People are happy if they can do what they think is right without feeling guilty.

Romans 14:22 NCV

The fear of human opinion disables; trusting in God protects you from that.

Proverbs 29:25 MSG

A Timely Tip for Dads

You, too, may be caught up in the modern-day push toward perfection, and if you are, your attitude will be contagious. When you "lighten up" on yourself, you will, in turn, do the same for your children.

Some Very Bright Ideas

What makes a Christian a Christian is not perfection but forgiveness.

Max Lucado

We shall never come to the perfect man 'til we come to the perfect world.

Matthew Henry

Nothing would be done at all, if a man waited until he could do it so well that no one could find fault with it.

John Henry Cardinal Newman

A Father-Son Prayer

Dear Lord, help us remember that we don't have to be perfect. We will try hard to be a good people, Lord, but we won't expect to be perfect people. Amen

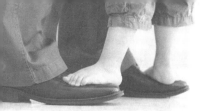

Devo 15

Right and Wrong

Lead a tranquil and quiet life in all godliness and dignity.

1 Timothy 2:2 HCSB

If you're old enough to know right from wrong, then you're old enough to do something about it. In other words, you should always try to do the right thing, and you should also do your very best not to do the wrong thing.

The more self-control you have, the easier it is to do the right thing. Why? Because, when you learn to think first and do things next, you avoid lots of silly mistakes. So here's great advice: first, slow down long enough to figure out the right thing to do—and then do it. You'll make yourself happy, and you'll make lots of other people happy, too.

A Timely Tip for Boys

Good behavior leads to a happy life. And bad behavior doesn't. Behave accordingly.

More from God's Word

As obedient children, do not be conformed to the desires of your former ignorance but, as the One who called you is holy, you also are to be holy in all your conduct.

1 Peter 1:14-15 HCSB

For this very reason, make every effort to supplement your faith with goodness, goodness with knowledge, knowledge with self-control, self-control with endurance, endurance with godliness.

2 Peter 1:5-6 HCSB

Therefore as you have received Christ Jesus the Lord, walk in Him.

Colossians 2:6 HCSB

A Timely Tip for Dads

When talking to your children about God, your actions speak much more loudly than your words. So behave accordingly.

Some Very Bright Ideas

The best evidence of our having the truth is our walking in the truth.

Matthew Henry

Study the Bible and observe how the persons behaved and how God dealt with them. There is explicit teaching on every condition of life.

Corrie ten Boom

I have found that the closer I am to the godly people around me, the easier it is for me to live a righteous life because they hold me accountable.

John MacArthur

A Father-Son Prayer

Dear Lord, there is a right way and a wrong way to live. Teach us the right way to live, Lord, this day and every day. Amen

Yes, Jesus Loves You

Just as the Father has loved Me, I also have loved you. Remain in My love.

John 15:9 HCSB

The Bible makes this promise: Jesus loves you. And how should that make you feel? Well, the fact that Jesus loves you should make you very happy indeed, so happy, in fact, that you try your best to do the things that Jesus wants you to do.

Jesus wants you to welcome Him into your heart, He wants you to love and obey God, and He wants you to be kind to people. These are all very good things to do . . . and the rest is up to you!

A Timely Tip for Boys

Jesus loves you so much that He gave His life so that you might live forever with Him in heaven. And how can you repay Christ's love? By accepting Him into your heart and by obeying His rules. When you do, He will love you and bless you today, tomorrow, and forever.

More from God's Word

And I am convinced that nothing can ever separate us from his love. Whether we are high above the sky or in the deepest ocean, nothing in all creation will ever be able to separate us from the love of God that is revealed in Christ Jesus our Lord.

Romans 8:38–39 NLT

And remember, I am with you always, to the end of the age.

Matthew 28:20 HCSB

I am the good shepherd. The good shepherd lays down his life for the sheep.

John 10:11 HCSB

A Timely Tip for Dads

Through His sacrifice on the cross, Jesus demonstrated His love for you and your child. As a responsible parent, it's up to you to make certain your youngster understands that Christ's love changes everything.

Some Very Bright Ideas

No man ever loved like Jesus. He taught the blind to see and the dumb to speak. He died on the cross to save us. He bore our sins. And now God says, "Because He did, I can forgive you."

Billy Graham

The richest meaning of your life is contained in the idea that Christ loved you enough to give His life for you.

Calvin Miller

Jesus is all compassion. He never betrays us.

Catherine Marshall

A Father-Son Prayer

Dear Jesus, we thank You for Your love, a love that never ends. We will return Your love, and we will share it with the world. Amen

Respecting Others

Just as you want others to do for you, do the same for them.

Luke 6:31 HCSB

How should you treat other people? Jesus has the answer to that question. Jesus wants you to treat other people exactly like you want to be treated: with kindness, respect, and courtesy. When you do, you'll make your family and friends happy . . . and that's what God wants.

So if you're wondering how to treat someone else, follow the Golden Rule: treat the other people like you want them to treat you. When you do, you'll be obeying your Father in heaven and you'll be making other folks happy at the same time.

A Timely Tip for Boys

When dealing with other people, it is important to try to walk in their shoes.

More from God's Word

See that no one renders evil for evil to anyone, but always pursue what is good both for yourselves and for all.

1 Thessalonians 5:15 NKJV

If you really carry out the royal law prescribed in Scripture, You shall love your neighbor as yourself, you are doing well.

James 2:8 HCSB

And let us not grow weary while doing good, for in due season we shall reap if we do not lose heart.

Galatians 6:9 NKJV

A Timely Tip for Dads

Kids imitate parents, so act accordingly! The best way for your child to learn the Golden Rule is by example . . . your example!

Some Very Bright Ideas

Anything done for another is done for oneself.

Pope John Paul II

To keep the Golden Rule we must put ourselves in other people's places, but to do that consists in and depends upon picturing ourselves in their places.

Harry Emerson Fosdick

It is wrong for anyone to be anxious to receive more from his neighbor than he himself is willing to give to God.

St. Francis of Assisi

A Father-Son Prayer

Dear Lord, help us always to do our very best to treat others as we wish to be treated. The Golden Rule is Your rule, Father. we will make it our rule, too. Amen

Devo 18

Changing Habits

Do not be deceived: "Evil company corrupts good habits."
1 Corinthians 15:33 NKJV

Most boys have a few habits they'd like to change, and maybe you do, too. If so, God can help.

If you trust God, and if you keep asking Him to help you change bad habits, He will help you make yourself into a new person. So, if at first you don't succeed, keep praying. God is listening, and He's ready to help you be a better person if you ask Him . . . so ask Him!

A Timely Tip for Boys

The old saying is familiar and true: "First you make your habits; then your habits make you." So it's always a good time to ask this question: "What kind of person are my habits making me?"

More from God's Word

Above all else, guard your heart, for it affects everything you do.
Proverbs 4:23 NLT

The peace of God, which surpasses all understanding, will guard your hearts and minds through Christ Jesus.
Philippians 4:7 NKJV

Don't copy the behavior and customs of this world, but let God transform you into a new person by changing the way you think. Then you will know what God wants you to do, and you will know how good and pleasing and perfect his will really is.
Romans 12:2 NLT

A Timely Tip for Dads

Target your most unhealthy habit first, and attack it with vigor. When it comes to defeating harmful habitual behaviors, you'll need focus, determination, prayer, more focus, more determination, and more prayer.

Some Very Bright Ideas

You will never change your life until you change something you do daily.

John Maxwell

Because bad habits are highly contagious, you should select only those friends whose habits you'd be happy to acquire.

Criswell Freeman

The simple fact is that if we sow a lifestyle that is in direct disobedience to God's Word, we ultimately reap disaster.

Charles Swindoll

A Father-Son Prayer

Dear Lord, please help us do things that are pleasing to You, and help us form habits that are pleasing to You. Amen

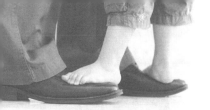

Always Be Honest

The honest person will live safely, but the one who is dishonest will be caught.

Proverbs 10:9 ICB

Nobody can tell the truth for you. You're the one who decides what you are going to say. You're the one who decides whether your words will be truthful . . . or not.

The word "integrity" means doing the right and honest thing. If you're going to be a person of integrity, it's up to you. If you want to live a life that is pleasing to God and to others, make integrity a habit. When you do, everybody wins, especially you!

A Timely Tip for Boys

Unless you build your friendships on honesty, you're building on a slippery slope.

More from God's Word

How happy are those whose way is blameless, who live according to the law of the Lord! Happy are those who keep His decrees and seek Him with all their heart.

Psalm 119:1-2 HCSB

Therefore laying aside falsehood, speak truth, each one of you, with his neighbor, for we are members of one another.

Ephesians 4:25 NASB

But when he, the Spirit of truth, comes, he will guide you into all truth....

John 16:13 NIV

A Timely Tip for Dads

Teach the importance of integrity every day, and, if necessary, use words.

Some Very Bright Ideas

A lie is like a snowball: the further you roll it, the bigger it becomes.

Martin Luther

God doesn't expect you to be perfect, but he does insist on complete honesty.

Rick Warren

You cannot glorify Christ and practice deception at the same time.

Warren Wiersbe

A Father-Son Prayer

Dear Lord, You have given us so many reasons to be happy. Every day, we will try to be joyful Christians as we give thanks for Your gifts, for Your love, and for Your Son. Amen

Kindness Starts with You

Be kind to one another, tender-hearted, forgiving each other, just as God in Christ also has forgiven you.

Ephesians 4:32 NASB

If you're waiting for other people to be nice to you before you're nice to them, you've got it backwards. Kindness starts with you! You see, you can never control what other people will say or do, but you can control your own behavior.

The Bible tells us that we should never stop doing good deeds as long as we live. Kindness is God's way, and it should be our way, too.

A Timely Tip for Boys

In order to be a kind person, you must do kind things. Thinking about them isn't enough. So get busy! Your family and friends need all the kindness they can get!

More from God's Word

Love is patient; love is kind.

1 Corinthians 13:4 HCSB

And may the Lord make you increase and abound in love to one another and to all.

1 Thessalonians 3:12 NKJV

Pure and undefiled religion before our God and Father is this: to look after orphans and widows in their distress and to keep oneself unstained by the world.

James 1:27 HCSB

A Timely Tip for Dads

Kindness is contagious; kids can catch it from their parents.

Some Very Bright Ideas

No one heals himself by wounding another.

St. Ambrose

The nicest thing we can do for our heavenly Father is to be kind to one of His children.

St. Teresa of Avila

When you extend hospitality to others, you're not trying to impress people, you're trying to reflect God to them.

Max Lucado

A Father-Son Prayer

Dear Lord, we know that You want us to be kind. Help us be kind today, tomorrow, and every day after that. Amen

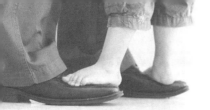

Perfect Love

For God so loved the world that he gave his only Son, so that everyone who believes in him will not perish but have eternal life.

John 3:16 NLT

The Bible makes this promise: God is love. It's a big promise, a very important description of what God is and how God works. God's love is perfect. When we open our hearts to His love, we are blessed and we are protected.

Tonight, offer sincere prayers of thanksgiving to your Heavenly Father. He loves you now and throughout all eternity. Open your heart to His presence and His love.

A Timely Tip for Boys

When you learn about the Bible, you'll learn how much God loves you.

More from God's Word

Unfailing love surrounds those who trust the LORD.

Psalm 32:10 NLT

For the LORD your God has arrived to live among you. He is a mighty savior. He will rejoice over you with great gladness. With his love, he will calm all your fears. He will exult over you by singing a happy song.

Zephaniah 3:17 NLT

But God demonstrates His own love toward us, in that while we were still sinners, Christ died for us.

Romans 5:8 NKJV

A Timely Tip for Dads

God's love for you is too big to understand, but it's not too big to share.

Some Very Bright Ideas

Love has its source in God, for love is the very essence of His being.

Kay Arthur

Jesus: the proof of God's love.

Philip Yancey

Though our feelings come and go, God's love for us does not.

C. S. Lewis

A Father-Son Prayer

Dear Lord, You are the truth and the light. Today and every day, we will make You our truth and our light. Amen

The Best Excuse Is No Excuse

Each of us will be rewarded for his own hard work.

1 Corinthians 3:8 TLB

What is an excuse? Well, when you make up an excuse, that means that you try to come up with a good reason that you didn't do something that you should have done.

Anybody can make up excuses, and you can too. But you shouldn't get into the habit of making too many excuses. Why? Because excuses don't work. And why don't they work? Because everybody has already heard so many excuses that almost everybody can recognize excuses when they hear them.

So the next time you're tempted to make up an excuse, don't. Instead of making an excuse, do what you think is right. After all, the very best excuse . . . is no excuse.

A Timely Tip for Boys

The habit of making excuses is a bad habit. Excuses lead to trouble. If you're in the habit of making excuses, the best day to stop that habit is today.

More from God's Word

It is God's will that your good lives should silence those who make foolish accusations against you. You are not slaves; you are free. But your freedom is not an excuse to do evil. You are free to live as God's slaves.

1 Peter 2:15-16 NLT

You can be sure that no immoral, impure, or greedy person will inherit the Kingdom of Christ and of God. For a greedy person is really an idolater who worships the things of this world. Don't be fooled by those who try to excuse these sins, for the terrible anger of God comes upon all those who disobey him.

Ephesians 5:5-6 NLT

Let us live in a right way . . . clothe yourselves with the Lord Jesus Christ and forget about satisfying your sinful self.

Romans 13:13-14 NCV

A Timely Tip for Dads

As a parent, you may hear lots and lots of excuses, some of which are valid, but many of which are not. It's your job to determine the difference between valid excuses and imaginary ones, and then to help your child understand the difference between the two.

Some Very Bright Ideas

Making up a string of excuses is usually harder than doing the work.

Marie T. Freeman

Replace your excuses with fresh determination.

Charles Swindoll

Never use your problem as an excuse for bad attitudes or behavior.

Joyce Meyer

A Father-Son Prayer

Dear Lord, when we are tempted to make excuses, help us to be strong as we accept responsibility for our actions. Amen

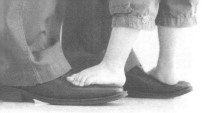

Devo 23

How Would He Behave?

*And he saith unto them, follow me, and I will make you fishers
of men. And they straightway left their nets, and followed him.*
Matthew 4:19-20 KJV

If Jesus were here, how would He behave? He would be
loving and forgiving. He would worship God with sincere
devotion. He would serve other people, and He would always abide by the Golden Rule. If Jesus were here, He would
stand up for truth and speak out against evil.

We read in the Bible that Jesus wants each of us to do
our best to be like Him. We can't be perfect Christians, but
we can do our best to obey God's commandments and to follow Christ's example. When we do so, we bring honor to the
One who gave His life for each of us.

A Timely Tip for Boys

When you have an important decision to make, stop for a
minute and think about how Jesus would behave if He were
in your shoes.

More from God's Word

Walk in a manner worthy of the God who calls you into His own kingdom and glory.

1 Thessalonians 2:12 NASB

And you shall do what is right and good in the sight of the Lord, that it may be well with you.

Deuteronomy 6:18 NKJV

I, therefore, the prisoner in the Lord, urge you to walk worthy of the calling you have received.

Ephesians 4:1 HCSB

A Timely Tip for Dads

Kids often imitate their parents, so act accordingly! The best way for your children to learn how to follow in Christ's footsteps is by following you while you follow Him!

Some Very Bright Ideas

He leads us in the paths of righteousness wherever we are placed.

Oswald Chambers

The best evidence of our having the truth is our walking in the truth.

Matthew Henry

Life is a series of choices between the bad, the good, and the best. Everything depends on how we choose.

Vance Havner

A Father-Son Prayer

Heavenly Father, we give thanks for our church and for the opportunity to worship there. Amen

A Pleasing Attitude

Set your minds on what is above, not on what is on the earth.

Colossians 3:2 HCSB

God knows everything about you, including your attitude. And when your attitude is good, God is pleased . . . very pleased.

Are you interested in pleasing God? Are you interested in pleasing your parents? Your teachers? And your friends? If so, try to make your attitude the best it can be. When you try hard to have a good attitude, you'll make other people feel better—and you'll make yourself feel better, too.

A Timely Tip for Boys

Remember that you can choose to have a good attitude or a not-so good attitude. And it's a choice you make every day.

More from God's Word

For the word of God is living and powerful, and sharper than any two-edged sword, piercing even to the division of soul and spirit, and of joints and marrow, and is a discerner of the thoughts and intents of the heart.

Hebrews 4:12 NKJV

Make your own attitude that of Christ Jesus.

Philippians 2:5 HCSB

Don't work only while being watched, in order to please men, but as slaves of Christ, do God's will from your heart. Render service with a good attitude, as to the Lord and not to men.

Ephesians 6:6-7 HCSB

A Timely Tip for Dads

A positive outlook on life is contagious. Your children can catch it from you . . . and they should!

Some Very Bright Ideas

I could go through this day oblivious to the miracles all around me, or I could tune in and "enjoy."

Gloria Gaither

The mind is like a clock that is constantly running down. It has to be wound up daily with good thoughts.

Fulton J. Sheen

You've heard the saying, "Life is what you make it." That means we have a choice. We can choose to have a life full of frustration and fear, but we can just as easily choose one of joy and contentment.

Dennis Swanberg

A Father-Son Prayer

Dear Lord, we pray for an attitude that pleases You. Even when we're angry, unhappy, tired, or upset, let us remember what it means to be good people and good Christians. Amen

Your Most Important Book

But grow in the grace and knowledge of our Lord and Savior Jesus Christ. To Him be the glory both now and forever. Amen.

2 Peter 3:18 NKJV

What book contains everything that God has to say about His rules and His Son? The Bible, of course. If you read the Bible every day, you'll soon learn how God wants you to behave.

Since doing the right thing (and the smart thing) is important to God, it should be important to you, too. And you'll learn what's right by reading the Bible.

The Bible is the most important book you'll ever own. It's God's Holy Word. Read it every day, and follow its instructions. When you do, you'll be safe now and forever.

A Timely Tip for Boys

Try to read your Bible with your parents every day. If they forget, remind them!

More from God's Word

There's nothing like the written Word of God for showing you the way to salvation through faith in Christ Jesus. Every part of Scripture is God-breathed and useful one way or another, showing us truth, exposing our rebellion, correcting our mistakes, training us to live God's way. Through the Word we are put together and shaped up for the tasks God has for us.

2 Timothy 3:15-17 MSG

For I am not ashamed of the gospel of Christ, for it is the power of God to salvation for everyone who believes.

Romans 1:16 NKJV

But the man who looks intently into the perfect law that gives freedom, and continues to do this, not forgetting what he has heard, but doing it—he will be blessed in what he does.

James 1:25 NIV

A Timely Tip for Dads

Never stop studying God's Word. Even if you've been studying the Bible for many years, you've still got lots to learn. Bible study should be a lifelong endeavor; make it your lifelong endeavor.

Some Very Bright Ideas

If one examines the secret behind a championship football team, a magnificent orchestra, or a successful business, the principal ingredient is invariably discipline.

James Dobson

Obedience to God is our job. The results of that obedience are God's.

Elisabeth Elliot

Hoping for a good future without investing in today is like a farmer waiting for a crop without ever planting any seed.

John Maxwell

A Father-Son Prayer

Dear Lord, the Bible teaches us that it's good to be in control of our emotions and our actions. So help us slow down, Lord, so we can look before we leap and think before we act. Amen

When Nobody Is Watching

Moderation is better than muscle, self-control better than political power.

Proverbs 16:32 MSG

When your teachers or parents aren't watching, what should you do? The answer, of course, is that you should behave exactly like you would if they were watching you. But sometimes, you may be tempted to do otherwise.

When a parent steps away or a teacher looks away, you may be tempted to say something or do something that you would not do if they were standing right beside you. But remember this: when nobody's watching, it's up to you to control yourself. And that's exactly what everybody wants you to do: your teachers want you to control yourself, and so do your parents. And so, by the way, does God.

A Timely Tip for Boys

When you learn how to control yourself, you'll be happier . . . and your parents will be happier, too.

More from God's Word

God hasn't invited us into a disorderly, unkempt life but into something holy and beautiful—as beautiful on the inside as the outside.

1 Thessalonians 4:7 MSG

Discipline yourself for the purpose of godliness.

1 Timothy 4:7 NASB

So don't lose a minute in building on what you've been given, complementing your basic faith with good character, spiritual understanding, alert discipline, passionate patience, reverent wonder, warm friendliness, and generous love, each dimension fitting into and developing the others.

2 Peter 1:5-7 MSG

A Timely Tip for Dads

Be an example of self-control. When it comes to parenting, you can't really teach it if you won't really live it.

Some Very Bright Ideas

God nowhere tells us to give up things for the sake of giving them up. He tells us to give them up for the sake of the only thing worth having—life with Himself.

Oswald Chambers

Your thoughts are the determining factor as to whose mold you are conformed to. Control your thoughts and you control the direction of your life.

Charles Stanley

This is my song through endless ages: Jesus led me all the way.

Fanny Crosby

A Father-Son Prayer

Dear Lord, the Bible teaches us to be wise, not foolish. So help us slow down and think things through so we can make better decisions and fewer mistakes. Amen

God's House

For where two or three are gathered together in My name, I am there among them.

Matthew 18:20 HCSB

When your parents take you to church, are you pleased to go? Hopefully so. After all, church is a wonderful place to learn about God's rules.

The church belongs to God just as surely as you belong to God. That's why the church is a good place to learn about God and about His Son Jesus.

So when your mom and dad take you to church, remember this: church is a fine place to be . . . and you're lucky to be there.

A Timely Tip for Boys

Forget the excuses. If somebody starts making up reasons not to go to church, don't pay any attention . . . even if that person is you!

More from God's Word

And I also say to you that you are Peter, and on this rock I will build My church, and the forces of Hades will not overpower it. I will give you the keys of the kingdom of heaven, and whatever you bind on earth will have been bound in heaven, and whatever you loose on earth will have been loosed in heaven.

Matthew 16:18-19 HCSB

Now you are the body of Christ, and individual members of it.

1 Corinthians 12:27 HCSB

Be on guard for yourselves and for all the flock, among whom the Holy Spirit has appointed you as overseers, to shepherd the church of God, which He purchased with His own blood.

Acts 20:28 HCSB

A Timely Tip for Dads

Your attitude toward church will help determine your kids' attitude toward church . . . so celebrate accordingly!

Some Very Bright Ideas

Christians are like coals in a fire. Together they glow—apart they grow cold.

Anonymous

It has always been the work of the church to bring others to belief in Christ and to experience a personal relationship with Him.

Charles Stanley

A body of believers brought together to witness the talents of one man is not a church—it is a study in futility.

Charles Swindoll

A Father-Son Prayer

Dear Lord, we thank You for Your church. When we are in church, we will learn about Your promises. And when we leave church, we will carry Your message into the world. Amen

Keep the Peace

Love must be without hypocrisy. Detest evil; cling to what is good. Show family affection to one another with brotherly love. Outdo one another in showing honor.

Romans 12:9–10 HCSB

Sometimes, it's easiest to become angry with the people we love the most. After all, we know that they'll still love us no matter how angry we become. But while it's easy to become angry at home, it's usually wrong.

The next time you're tempted to become angry with a brother, or a sister, or a parent, remember that these are the people who love you more than anybody else! Then, calm down. Because peace is always beautiful, especially when it's peace at your house.

A Timely Tip for Boys

What if you're having real problems within your family? You've simply got to keep talking things over, even if it's hard. And, remember: what seems like a mountain today may turn out to be a molehill tomorrow.

More from God's Word

Their first responsibility is to show godliness at home and repay their parents by taking care of them. This is something that pleases God very much.

1 Timothy 5:4 NLT

Every kingdom divided against itself will be ruined, and every city or household divided against itself will not stand.

Matthew 12:25 NIV

You must choose for yourselves today whom you will serve . . . as for me and my family, we will serve the Lord.

Joshua 24:15 NCV

A Timely Tip for Dads

As the parent, it's up to you (not your child) to determine the focus of family life at your house. If you and your family members focus on God first, you're on the right track. If you're focused on other things first, it's time to step back and reorder your priorities.

Some Very Bright Ideas

The first essential for a happy home is love.

Billy Graham

Your family is a priceless gift from God . . . and He expects you to treat it that way.

Criswell Freeman

A home is a place where we find direction.

Gigi Graham Tchividjian

More than any other single factor in a person's formative years, family life forges character.

John Maxwell

A Father-Son Prayer

Dear Lord, You have given us a priceless gift: our family. We praise You, Father, for our loved ones and for Your beloved Son Jesus. Amen

The Very Best Time to Forgive Somebody Is Now

Working together with Him, we also appeal to you: "Don't receive God's grace in vain." For He says: In an acceptable time, I heard you, and in the day of salvation, I helped you. Look, now is the acceptable time; look, now is the day of salvation.

2 Corinthians 6:1-2 HCSB

When is the best time to forgive somebody? Well, as the old saying goes, there's no time like the present. So if you have somebody you need to forgive, why not forgive that person today?

Forgiving other people is one of the ways that we make ourselves feel better. So if you're still angry about something that somebody did, forgive that person right now. There is no better time.

A Timely Tip for Boys

When the Lord tells you it is time to do something (like forgive someone), the time to do it is now.

More from God's Word

The intense prayer of the righteous is very powerful.
James 5:16 HCSB

Rejoice in hope; be patient in affliction; be persistent in prayer.
Romans 12:12 HCSB

Let the words of my mouth and the meditation of my heart be acceptable in Your sight, O Lord, my strength and my Redeemer.
Psalm 19:14 NKJV

A Timely Tip for Dads

Be a model of forgiveness. If you want your children to learn the art of forgiveness, then you must master that art yourself. If you're able to forgive those who have hurt you and, by doing so, move on with your life, your kids will learn firsthand that forgiveness is God's way.

Some Very Bright Ideas

TGIF—Thank God I'm Forgiven.

Anonymous

God expects us to forgive others as He has forgiven us; we are to follow His example by having a forgiving heart.

Vonette Bright

Forgiveness is the final form of love.

Reinhold Niebuhr

A Father-Son Prayer

Dear Lord, please give us the wisdom to forgive other people. We have made mistakes, and You have forgiven us, Father. So we will be quick to forgive others. Amen

Let's Be Patient

Knowledge begins with respect for the Lord, but fools hate wisdom and self-control.

Proverbs 1:7 NCV

The Bible tells us that we should be patient with everybody, not just with parents, teachers, and friends. In the eyes of God, all people are very important, so we should treat them that way.

Of course it's easy to be nice to the people we want to impress, but what about everybody else? Jesus gave us clear instructions: He said that when we do a good deed for someone less fortunate than we are, we have also done a good deed for our Savior. And as Christians, that's exactly what we are supposed to do!

A Timely Tip for Boys

Speak respectfully to everybody, starting with parents, grandparents, teachers, and adults . . . but don't stop there. Be respectful of everybody, including yourself!

More from God's Word

Be completely humble and gentle; be patient, bearing with one another in love.

Ephesians 4:2 NIV

Wherefore seeing we also are compassed about with so great a cloud of witnesses, let us lay aside every weight, and the sin which doth so easily beset us, and let us run with patience the race that is set before us....

Hebrews 12:1 KJV

Encourage each other. Live in harmony and peace. Then the God of love and peace will be with you.

2 Corinthians 13:11 NLT

A Timely Tip for Dads

Kindness, dignity, and respect for others begins at the head of the household and works its way down from there.

Some Very Bright Ideas

If you are willing to honor a person out of respect for God, you can be assured that God will honor you.

Beth Moore

How wonderful it is when parents and children respect each other . . . and show it.

Jim Gallery

It is my calling to treat every human being with grace and dignity, to treat every person, whether encountered in a palace or a gas station, as a life made in the image of God.

Sheila Walsh

A Father-Son Prayer

Dear Lord, help us learn to respect all people, starting with our family and our friends. And help us learn to treat other people in the same way that we want to be treated. Amen

Yes, Jesus Loves You!

*You're blessed when you're content with just who you are—
no more, no less. That's the moment you find yourselves proud
owners of everything that can't be bought.*

Matthew 5:5 MSG

Have you heard the song "Jesus Loves Me"? Probably so. It's a happy song that should remind you of this important fact: Jesus loves you very much.

When you invite Jesus into your heart, He'll protect you forever. If you have problems, He'll help you solve them. When you aren't perfect, He'll still love you. If you feel sorry or sad, He can help you feel better.

Yes, Jesus loves you . . . and you should love yourself. So the next time you feel sad about yourself . . . or something that you've done . . . remember that Jesus loves you, your family loves you, and you should feel that way, too.

A Timely Tip for Boys

Nobody else in the world is exactly like you. When God made you, He made a very special, one-of-a-kind person. So don't forget this fact: you're very, very, very special.

More from God's Word

For you made us only a little lower than God, and you crowned us with glory and honor.

Psalm 8:5 NLT

How happy are those whose way is blameless, who live according to the law of the Lord! Happy are those who keep His decrees and seek Him with all their heart.

Psalm 119:1-2 HCSB

Happy is the one whose help is the God of Jacob, whose hope is in the Lord his God.

Psalm 146:5 HCSB

A Timely Tip for Dads

If you want your child to admire the person he sees in the mirror, then you should do whatever it takes to be the kind of man who can admire the person he sees in the mirror.

Some Very Bright Ideas

Give yourself a gift today: be present with yourself. God is. Enjoy your own personality. God does.

Barbara Johnson

Even if you don't love yourself, God does. And He's right.

Criswell Freeman

Do not wish to be anything but what you are, and try to be that perfectly.

St. Francis of Sales

A Father-Son Prayer

Dear Lord, we have so much to learn and so many ways to improve ourselves. But You love us just as we are. Thank You, Father, for Your love and for Your Son. Amen

Friends Should Share

The righteous give without sparing.

Proverbs 21:26 NIV

H ow can you be a good friend? One way is by sharing. And here are some of the things you can share: smiles, kind words, pats on the back, your toys, school supplies, books, and, of course, your prayers.

Would you like to make your friends happy? And would you like to make yourself happy at the same time? Here's how: treat your friends like you want to be treated. That means obeying the Golden Rule, which, of course, means sharing. In fact, the more you share, the better friend you'll be.

A Timely Tip for Boys

Sharing with guests is an important way to demonstrate hospitality.

More from God's Word

The one who has two shirts must share with someone who has none, and the one who has food must do the same.

Luke 3:11 HCSB

Take heed that you do not do your charitable deeds before men, to be seen by them. Otherwise you have no reward in heaven.

Matthew 6:1 NKJV

If a brother or sister is without clothes and lacks daily food, and one of you says to them, "Go in peace, keep warm, and eat well," but you don't give them what the body needs, what good is it?

James 2:15–16 HCSB

A Timely Tip for Dads

It's almost Biblical: when two or more small children are gathered together, they are bound to fuss over toys. Use these disagreements as opportunities to preach the gospel of sharing (even if your sermon falls upon inattentive little ears!).

Some Very Bright Ideas

Don't be afraid to share what you have with others; after all, it all belongs to God anyway.

Jim Gallery

We are never more like God than when we give.

Charles Swindoll

Abundant living means abundant giving.

E. Stanley Jones

A Father-Son Prayer

Dear Lord, Jesus served others; we can too. So, we will share our possessions and our prayers. And, we will share kind words with our family and our friends. Amen

Devo 33

Avoiding Mischief

Therefore as you have received Christ Jesus the Lord, walk in Him.

Colossians 2:6 HCSB

Face facts: not everybody you know is well behaved. Your first job is to recognize bad behavior when you see it . . . and your second job is to make sure that you don't join in!

The moment that you decide to avoid mischief whenever you see it is the moment that you'll make yourself happy, your parents happy, and God happy. And you'll stay out of trouble. And you'll be glad you did!

A Timely Tip for Boys

Start now. If you really want to become a well-behaved person, the best day to get started is this one.

More from God's Word

Don't be deceived: God is not mocked. For whatever a man sows he will also reap, because the one who sows to his flesh will reap corruption from the flesh, but the one who sows to the Spirit will reap eternal life from the Spirit.

Galatians 6:7-8 HCSB

Who is wise and understanding among you? He should show his works by good conduct with wisdom's gentleness.

James 3:13 HCSB

Even a young man is known by his actions—by whether his behavior is pure and upright.

Proverbs 20:11 HCSB

A Timely Tip for Dads

Be disciplined in your own approach to life. You can't teach it if you won't live it.

Some Very Bright Ideas

Christians are the citizens of heaven, and while we are on earth, we ought to behave like heaven's citizens.

Warren Wiersbe

More depends on my walk than my talk.

D. L. Moody

Although God causes all things to work together for good for His children, He still holds us accountable for our behavior.

Kay Arthur

A Father-Son Prayer

Dear Lord, let us find ways to help other people. Jesus served others; we can too. We can share our possessions and our prayers. And, we can share kind words with our family and friends, today and every day. Amen

Big Rewards When You Do the Right Thing

Do you want to be counted wise, to build a reputation for wisdom? Here's what you do: Live well, live wisely, live humbly. It's the way you live, not the way you talk, that counts.

James 3:13 MSG

If you open up a dictionary, you'll see that the word "wisdom" means "using good judgement, and knowing what is true," But there's more to it than that. It's not enough to know what's right—if you want to be wise, you must also do what's right.

The Bible promises that when you do smart things, you'll earn big rewards, so slow down and think about things *before* you do them, not after.

A Timely Tip for Boys

If you learn to control yourself, you'll be glad. If you can't learn to control yourself, you'll be sad.

More from God's Word

Teach me, O Lord, the way of Your statutes, and I shall keep it to the end.

Psalm 119:33 NKJV

So teach us to number our days, that we may gain a heart of wisdom.

Psalm 90:12 NKJV

Acquire wisdom—how much better it is than gold! And acquire understanding—it is preferable to silver.

Proverbs 16:16 HCSB

A Timely Tip for Dads

Being a wise parent requires more than knowledge. Knowledge comes from text books, but wisdom comes from God. Wisdom begins with a thorough understanding of God's moral order, the eternal truths that are found in God's Holy Word.

Some Very Bright Ideas

This is the secret to a lifestyle of worship—doing everything as if you were doing it for Jesus.

Rick Warren

Knowledge can be found in books or in school. Wisdom, on the other hand, starts with God . . . and ends there.

Marie T. Freeman

The more wisdom enters our hearts, the more we will be able to trust our hearts in difficult situations.

John Eldredge

A Father-Son Prayer

Dear Lord, let us be patient with other people's mistakes, and let us be patient with our own mistakes. We know that we still have so many things to learn. So we won't stop learning; we won't give up; and we won't stop growing. Amen

Your Family Is a Gift

Love must be without hypocrisy. Detest evil; cling to what is good. Show family affection to one another with brotherly love. Outdo one another in showing honor.

Romans 12:9–10 HCSB

Your family is a wonderful, one-of-a-kind gift from God. And your family members love you very much—what a blessing it is to be loved!

Have you ever really stopped to think about how much you are loved? Your parents love you (of course) and so does everybody else in your family. But it doesn't stop there. You're also an important part of God's family . . . and He loves you more than you can imagine.

What should you do about all the love that comes your way? You should accept it; you should be thankful for it; and you should share it . . . starting now!

A Timely Tip for Boys

It's good to tell your loved ones how you feel about them, but that's not enough. You should also show them how you feel with your good deeds and your kind words.

More from God's Word

If I speak the languages of men and of angels, but do not have love, I am a sounding gong or a clanging cymbal.

1 Corinthians 13:1 HCSB

Now these three remain: faith, hope, and love. But the greatest of these is love.

1 Corinthians 13:13 HCSB

Dear friends, if God loved us in this way, we also must love one another.

1 John 4:11 HCSB

A Timely Tip for Dads

Be expressive. Your children desperately need to hear that you love them . . . from you! If you're bashful, shy, or naturally uncommunicative, get over it.

Some Very Bright Ideas

I like to think of my family as a big, beautiful patchwork quilt—each of us so different yet stitched together by love and life experiences.

Barbara Johnson

Life is a journey, and love is what makes that journey worthwhile.

Anonymous

Only God can give us a selfless love for others, as the Holy Spirit changes us from within.

Billy Graham

A Father-Son Prayer

Dear Lord, You have given us a family that cares for us and loves us. Thank You. We will let our family know that we love them by the things that we say and do. You know that we love our family, Lord. Now it's our turn to show them! Amen

Everybody Makes Mistakes

Instead, God has chosen the world's foolish things to shame the wise, and God has chosen the world's weak things to shame the strong.

1 Corinthians 1:27 HCSB

Do you make mistakes? Of course you do . . . everybody does. When you make a mistake, you must try your best to learn from it so that you won't make the very same mistake again. And, if you have hurt someone—or if you have disobeyed God—you must ask for forgiveness.

Remember: mistakes are a part of life, but the biggest mistake you can make is to keep making the same mistake over and over and over again.

A Timely Tip for Boys

If you make a mistake, the time to make things better is now, not later! The sooner you admit your mistake, the better.

More from God's Word

If you hide your sins, you will not succeed. If you confess and reject them, you will receive mercy.

Proverbs 28:13 NCV

If you listen to constructive criticism, you will be at home among the wise.

Proverbs 15:31 NLT

If we confess our sins to him, he is faithful and just to forgive us and to cleanse us from every wrong.

1 John 1:9 NLT

A Timely Tip for Dads

Even your own angelic child may make a mistake on occasion. When the unlikely happens, help your boy understand why the behavior is wrong and how to prevent it in the future.

Some Very Bright Ideas

I hope you don't mind me telling you all this. One can learn only by seeing one's mistakes.

C. S. Lewis

Father, take our mistakes and turn them into opportunities.

Max Lucado

God doesn't expect you to live a mistake-free life—and neither should you.

Criswell Freeman

A Father-Son Prayer

Dear Lord, sometimes we make mistakes. When we do, forgive us, Father. And help us learn from our mistakes so that we can be better people and better examples to our friends and family. Amen

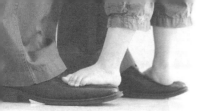

God's Power

I pray...that you may know...his uncomparably great power for us who believe....

Ephesians 1:18-19 NIV

How strong is God? Stronger than anybody can imagine! But even if we can't understand God's power, we can respect His power. And we can be sure that God has the strength to guide us and protect us forever.

The next time you're worried or afraid, remember this: if God is powerful enough to create the universe and everything in it, He's also strong enough to take care of you. Now that's a comforting thought!

A Timely Tip for Boys

When you place your faith in God, life becomes a grand adventure energized by His power.

More from God's Word

But Jesus looked at them and said, "With men this is impossible, but with God all things are possible."

Matthew 19:26 HCSB

You are the God who works wonders; You revealed Your strength among the peoples.

Psalm 77:14 HCSB

Ah, Lord God! Behold, You have made the heavens and the earth by Your great power and outstretched arm. There is nothing too hard for You.

Jeremiah 32:17 NKJV

A Timely Tip for Dads

You know that God is sovereign and that His power is unlimited. Make sure that your son knows it, too.

Some Very Bright Ideas

The power of God through His Spirit will work within us to the degree that we permit it.

Mrs. Charles E. Cowman

The impossible is exactly what God does.

Oswald Chambers

Our God is an awesome God; He reigns from heaven above with wisdom, power, and love.

Rich Mullins

A Father-Son Prayer

Dear God, Your power is far too great for us to understand. But we can sense Your presence and Your love every day of our lives—and that's exactly what we will try to do! Amen

Becoming a More Patient Person

Be gentle to all, able to teach, patient.

2 Timothy 2:24 NKJV

The Book of Proverbs tells us that patience is a very good thing. But for most of us, patience can also be a very hard thing. After all, we have many things that we want, and we want them NOW! But the Bible tells us that we must learn to wait patiently for the things that God has in store for us.

Are you having trouble being patient? If so, remember that patience takes practice, and lots of it, so keep trying. And if you make a mistake, don't be too upset. After all, if you're going to be a really patient person, you shouldn't just be patient with others, you should also be patient with yourself.

A Timely Tip for Boys

An important part of growing up is learning to be patient with others and with yourself. And one more thing: learn from everybody's mistakes, especially your own.

More from God's Word

Knowing God leads to self-control. Self-control leads to patient endurance, and patient endurance leads to godliness.

2 Peter 1:6 NLT

Patience and encouragement come from God. And I pray that God will help you all agree with each other the way Christ Jesus wants.

Romans 15:5 NCV

But if we look forward to something we don't have yet, we must wait patiently and confidently.

Romans 8:25 NLT

A Timely Tip for Dads

Kids imitate their parents, so act accordingly! The best way for your child to learn to be patient is by example . . . your example!

Some Very Bright Ideas

We are so used to living in an instant world that it is difficult to wait for anything.

Kay Arthur

Patience pays. Impatience costs.

Criswell Freeman

The challenge before us is to have faith in God, and the hardest part of faith is waiting.

Jim Cymbala

A Father-Son Prayer

Dear Lord, sometimes we are not as patient as we could be, or as patient as we should be. Please slow us down, Lord. And teach us to follow in the footsteps of Your Son today and every day. Amen

Devo 39

Working Together

Work at getting along with each other and with God. Otherwise you'll never get so much as a glimpse of God.

Hebrews 12:14 MSG

Helping other people can be fun! When you help others, you feel better about yourself—and you'll know that God approves of what you're doing.

When you learn how to cooperate with your family and friends, you'll soon discover that it's more fun when everybody works together.

So do everybody a favor: learn better ways to share and better ways to cooperate. It's the right thing to do.

A Timely Tip for Boys

Cooperation pays. When you cooperate with your friends and family, you'll feel good about yourself—and your family and friends will feel good about you, too.

More from God's Word

You're blessed when you can show people how to cooperate instead of compete or fight. That's when you discover who you really are, and your place in God's family.

Matthew 5:9 MSG

Be kind to each other, tenderhearted, forgiving one another, just as God through Christ has forgiven you.

Ephesians 4:32 NLT

Carry one another's burdens; in this way you will fulfill the law of Christ.

Galatians 6:2 HCSB

A Timely Tip for Dads

You know that your children can accomplish much more in life by working cooperatively with others. So it's up to you to teach the fine art of cooperation. And make no mistake: the best way to teach the art of cooperation is by example.

Some Very Bright Ideas

Coming together is a beginning. Keeping together is progress.
Working together is success.

John Maxwell

A friend is one who makes me do my best.

Oswald Chambers

One person working together doesn't accomplish much.
Success is the result of people pulling together to meet
common goals.

John Maxwell

A Father-Son Prayer

*Dear Lord, when we become upset, calm us down. When we
become angry, give us self-control. When we feel the urge to hurt
other people, let us remember that Jesus forgave other folks, and
we should, too. Amen*

Don't Copy Friends Who Misbehave

Stay away from a foolish man; you will gain no knowledge from his speech.

Proverbs 14:7 HCSB

If your friends misbehave, do you misbehave right along with them, or do you tell them to stop? Usually, it's much easier to go along with your friends, even if you know they're misbehaving. But it's always better to do the right thing, even if it's hard.

Sometimes, grownups must stand up for the things they believe in. When they do, it can be hard for them, too. But the Bible tells us over and over again that we should do the right thing, not the easy thing.

When your friends misbehave, it can spoil everything. So if your friends behave badly, don't copy them! And if your friends keep behaving badly, choose different friends.

A Timely Tip for Boys

Face facts: since you can't please everybody, you're better off trying to please the people who are trying to help you become a better person, not the people who are encouraging you to misbehave!

More from God's Word

My son, if sinners entice you, don't be persuaded.

Proverbs 1:10 HCSB

Blessed is the man who walks not in the counsel of the ungodly, nor stands in the path of sinners, nor sits in the seat of the scornful; but his delight is in the law of the Lord, and in His law he meditates day and night.

Psalm 1:1-2 NKJV

Do not be deceived: "Bad company corrupts good morals."

1 Corinthians 15:33 HCSB

A Timely Tip for Dads

Thoughtful Christian parents don't follow the crowd . . . thoughtful Christian parents follow Jesus.

Some Very Bright Ideas

Do you want to be wise? Choose wise friends.

Charles Swindoll

It's tempting to follow the crowd, but usually it's better to follow your conscience.

Criswell Freeman

There is nothing that makes more cowards and feeble men than public opinion.

Henry Ward Beecher

A Father-Son Prayer

Dear Lord, help us worry less about pleasing other people and more about pleasing You. Amen

Devo 41

Share Your Blessings

Remember this: the person who sows sparingly will also reap sparingly, and the person who sows generously will also reap generously.

2 Corinthians 9:6 HCSB

Jesus told us that we should be generous with other people, but sometimes we don't feel much like sharing. Instead of sharing the things that we have, we want to keep them all to ourselves. But God doesn't want selfishness to rule our hearts; He wants us to be generous.

Are you lucky enough to have nice things? If so, God's instructions are clear: you must share your blessings with others. And that's exactly the way it should be. After all, think how generous God has been with you.

A Timely Tip for Boys

There is a direct relationship between generosity and joy— the more you give to others, the more joy you will experience for yourself.

More from God's Word

When it is in your power, don't withhold good from the one to whom it is due.

Proverbs 3:27 HCSB

So whenever you give to the poor, don't sound a trumpet before you, as the hypocrites do in the synagogues and on the streets, to be applauded by people. I assure you: They've got their reward! But when you give to the poor, don't let your left hand know what your right hand is doing, so that your giving may be in secret. And your Father who sees in secret will reward you.

Matthew 6:2-4 HCSB

A generous person will be enriched.

Proverbs 11:25 HCSB

A Timely Tip for Dads

Being kind is a learned behavior. You're the teacher. Class is in session. Your child is in attendance. Actions speak louder than words. And it's one of the most important courses you will ever teach.

Some Very Bright Ideas

How generous you are does not depend on how much you give, but how much you have left.

Anonymous

If you want to be truly happy, you won't find it on an endless quest for more stuff. You'll find it in receiving God's generosity and in passing that generosity along.

Bill Hybels

Part of everything we have is ours to give away.

Mary Hunt

A Father-Son Prayer

Dear Lord, help us be a generous and cheerful. Let us find ways to serve others, and let us find encouraging words to share with people who need our help. Amen

Draw a Picture Together about Sharing

Devo 42

Is the Golden Rule Your Rule, Too?

Don't be selfish.... Be humble, thinking of others as better than yourself.

Philippians 2:3 TLB

Is the Golden Rule your rule, or is it just another Bible verse that goes in one ear and out the other? Jesus made Himself perfectly clear: He instructed you to treat other people in the same way that you want to be treated. But sometimes, especially when you're feeling pressure from friends, or when you're tired or upset, obeying the Golden Rule can seem like an impossible task—but it's not. So be kind to everybody and obey God's rule, the Golden Rule, that is.

A Timely Tip for Boys

You must do more than talk about it. In order to be a good person, you must do good things. So get busy! The best time to do a good deed is as soon as you can do it!

More from God's Word

Each of you should look not only to your own interests, but also to the interest of others.

Philippians 2:4 NIV

Carry each other's burdens, and in this way you will fulfill the law of Christ.

Galatians 6:2 NIV

See that no one renders evil for evil to anyone, but always pursue what is good both for yourselves and for all.

1 Thessalonians 5:15 NKJV

A Timely Tip for Dads

The Golden Rule is as good as gold—in fact, it's better than gold. And as a responsible parent, you should make certain that your child knows that the Golden Rule is, indeed, golden.

Some Very Bright Ideas

The Golden Rule starts at home, but it should never stop there.

Marie T. Freeman

It is one of the most beautiful compensations of life that no one can sincerely try to help another without helping herself.

Barbara Johnson

The #1 rule of friendship is the Golden one.

Jim Gallery

A Father-Son Prayer

Dear Lord, the Golden Rule is Your rule. Today and every day, we will try to make it our rule, too. Amen

Devo 43

White Lies?

Doing what is right brings freedom to honest people.

Proverbs 11:6 ICB

Sometimes, people convince themselves that it's okay to tell "little white lies." Sometimes people convince themselves that itsy bitsy lies aren't harmful. But there's a problem: little lies have a way of growing into big ones, and once they grow up, they cause lots of problems.

Remember that lies, no matter what size, are not part of God's plan for our lives, so tell the truth about everything. It's the right thing to do, and besides: when you always tell the truth, you don't have to try and remember what you said!

A Timely Tip for Boys

Never be afraid to tell the truth. Even when the truth hurts, telling the truth is better than telling a lie. Far better!

More from God's Word

Ye shall not steal, neither deal falsely, neither lie one to another.
Leviticus 19:11 KJV

The one who lives with integrity lives securely, but whoever perverts his ways will be found out.
Proverbs 10:9 HCSB

The one who lives with integrity will be helped, but one who distorts right and wrong will suddenly fall.
Proverbs 28:18 HCSB

A Timely Tip for Dads

Telling the truth isn't just hard for kids; it can be hard for parents, too. And when honesty is hard, that's precisely the moment when wise parents remember that their children are watching . . . and learning.

Some Very Bright Ideas

The single most important element in any human relationship is honesty—with oneself, with God, and with others.

Catherine Marshall

Integrity is not a given factor in everyone's life. It is a result of self-discipline, inner trust, and a decision to be relentlessly honest in all situations in our lives.

John Maxwell

We can teach our children that being honest protects from guilt and provides for a clear conscience.

Josh McDowell

A Father-Son Prayer

Dear Lord, we want to be people whose words are true and whose hearts are pure. In everything that we do, let us use Jesus as our model and our guide. Amen

Hopes, Hopes, and More Hopes

Make me hear joy and gladness.

Psalm 51:8 NKJV

Hope is a very good thing to have . . . and to share. So make this promise to yourself and keep it: promise yourself that you'll be a hopeful person. Think good thoughts. Trust God. Become friends with Jesus. And trust your hopes, not your fears. Then, when you've filled your heart with hope and gladness, share your good thoughts with friends. They'll be better for it, and so will you.

A Timely Tip for Boys

Think about all the things you have (starting with your family and your faith) . . . and think about all the things you can do! Believe in yourself.

More from God's Word

I am able to do all things through Him who strengthens me.

Philippians 4:13 HCSB

But if we hope for what we do not see, we eagerly wait for it with patience.

Romans 8:25 HCSB

Lord, I turn my hope to You. My God, I trust in You.

Psalm 25:1-2 HCSB

A Timely Tip for Dads

Cynicism is contagious, and so is optimism. Raise your children accordingly.

Some Very Bright Ideas

The people whom I have seen succeed best in life have always been cheerful and hopeful people who went about their business with a smile on their faces.

Charles Kingsley

Developing a positive attitude means working continually to find what is uplifting and encouraging.

Barbara Johnson

There is wisdom in the habit of looking at the bright side of life.

Father Flanagan

A Father-Son Prayer

Dear Lord, You have given us so many things to be happy about. So, we will try our best to think good thoughts, and we will look for the best in other people, today and every day. Amen

Be Respectful

Show respect for all people. Love the brothers and sisters of God's family.

1 Peter 2:17 ICB

Are you polite and respectful to your parents and teachers? And do you do your best to treat everybody with the respect they deserve? If you want to obey God's rules, then you should be able to answer yes to these questions.

Remember this: the Bible teaches you to be a respectful person—and if it's right there in the Bible, it's certainly the right thing to do!

A Timely Tip for Boys

If you're angry with your mom or your dad, don't blurt out something unkind. If you can't say anything nice, go to your room and don't come out until you can.

More from God's Word

Therefore, God's chosen ones, holy and loved, put on heartfelt compassion, kindness, humility, gentleness, and patience.

Colossians 3:12 HCSB

Reverence for the Lord is the foundation of true wisdom. The rewards of wisdom come to all who obey him.

Psalm 111:10 NLT

Acquire wisdom—how much better it is than gold! And acquire understanding—it is preferable to silver.

Proverbs 16:16 HCSB

A Timely Tip for Dads

Children may seek to find humor in the misfortunes of others; children may, on occasion, exhibit cruelty towards other children. Be watchful for such behaviors and correct them with enthusiasm and vigor.

Some Very Bright Ideas

If you are willing to honor a person out of respect for God, you can be assured that God will honor you.

Beth Moore

If my heart is right with God, every human being is my neighbor.

Oswald Chambers

Use your head to handle yourself, your heart to handle others.

Anonymous

A Father-Son Prayer

Dear Lord, please give us the maturity to respect other people, today and every day. Amen

Your Continual Feast

A cheerful heart has a continual feast.

Proverbs 15:15 HCSB

What is a continual feast? It's a little bit like a non-stop birthday party: fun, fun, and more fun! The Bible tells us that a cheerful heart can make life like a continual feast, and that's something worth working for.

Where does cheerfulness begin? It begins inside each of us; it begins in the heart. So please be thankful to God for His blessings, and let's show our thanks by sharing good cheer wherever we go. This old world needs all the cheering up it can get . . . and so do we!

A Timely Tip for Boys

Cheer up somebody else. Do you need a little cheering up? If so, find somebody else who needs cheering up, too. Then, do your best to brighten that person's day. When you do, you'll discover that cheering up other people is a wonderful way to cheer yourself up, too!

More from God's Word

A merry heart does good, like medicine.

Proverbs 17:22 NKJV

Is anyone cheerful? He should sing praises.

James 5:13 HCSB

Make me hear joy and gladness.

Psalm 51:8 NKJV

A Timely Tip for Dads

Cheerfulness is an attitude that is highly contagious. Kids often catch it from their parents. Remember that cheerfulness starts at the top. A cheerful household usually begins with cheerful adults.

Some Very Bright Ideas

When we bring sunshine into the lives of others, we're warmed by it ourselves. When we spill a little happiness, it splashes on us.

Barbara Johnson

Cheerfulness prepares a glorious mind for all the noblest acts of religion—love, adoration, praise, and every union with our God.

St. Elizabeth Ann Seton

Sour godliness is the devil's religion.

John Wesley

A Father-Son Prayer

Dear Lord, we have so many blessings. Help us count those blessings and be glad. And, let Your love live in our hearts this day and forever. Amen

Sharing Your Stuff

In every way I've shown you that by laboring like this, it is necessary to help the weak and to keep in mind the words of the Lord Jesus, for He said, "It is more blessed to give than to receive."

Acts 20:35 HCSB

Are you one of those boys who is lucky enough to have a closet filled up with stuff? If so, it's probably time to share some of it.

When your mom or dad says it's time to clean up your closet and give some things away, don't be sad. Instead of whining, think about all the children who could enjoy the things that you don't use very much. And while you're at it, think about what Jesus might tell you to do if He were here. Jesus would tell you to share generously and cheerfully. And that's exactly what you should do!

A Timely Tip for Boys

Finding loving homes for your old clothes and toys. Your parents can help you find younger children who need the clothes and toys that you've outgrown.

More from God's Word

And above all things have fervent charity among yourselves: for charity shall cover the multitude of sins.

1 Peter 4:8 KJV

Instruct those who are rich in the present age not to be arrogant or to set their hope on the uncertainty of wealth, but on God, who richly provides us with all things to enjoy. Instruct them to do good, to be rich in good works, to be generous, willing to share.

1 Timothy 6:17-18 HCSB

Be generous: Invest in acts of charity. Charity yields high returns.

Ecclesiastes 11:1 MSG

A Timely Tip for Dads

When it comes to charity, consistency matters. Do something every day that helps another person have a better life.

Some Very Bright Ideas

Charity is the pure gold which makes us rich in eternal wealth.

Jean Pierre Camus

You can't read the Scriptures without being struck that over 2,500 verses deal with the sick, the hungry, the orphans.

Tony P. Hall

I never look at the masses as my responsibility. I look at the individual. I can love only one person at a time. I can feed only one person at a time. Just one, one, one. You get closer to Christ by coming closer to each other.

Mother Teresa

A Father-Son Prayer

Dear Lord, You've given our family so much, and we know we are blessed. Yet, there are so many people in this world who need our help. Give us the wisdom to share our blessings; let us be kind, generous, and helpful, this day and every day. Amen

What Kind of Example?

You are young, but do not let anyone treat you as if you were not important. Be an example to show the believers how they should live. Show them with your words, with the way you live, with your love, with your faith, and with your pure life.

1 Timothy 4:12 ICB

Like it or not, your behavior is a powerful example to others. The question is not whether you will be an example to your friends; the only question is this: What kind of example will you be?

Corrie ten Boom advised, "Don't worry about what you do not understand. Worry about what you do understand in the Bible but do not live by." And that's good advice because your family and friends are always watching . . . and so, for that matter, is God.

A Timely Tip for Boys

Don't exaggerate! All of us have enough troubles without pretending that we have more.

More from God's Word

Do everything without grumbling and arguing, so that you may be blameless and pure.

Philippians 2:14–15 HCSB

Set an example of good works yourself, with integrity and dignity in your teaching.

Titus 2:7 HCSB

For the kingdom of God is not in talk but in power.

1 Corinthians 4:20 HCSB

A Timely Tip for Dads

Give your children the gift of a lifetime. How? By being a worthy example.

Some Very Bright Ideas

One of the best ways to witness to family, friends, and neighbors is to let them see the difference Jesus has made in your life.

Anne Graham Lotz

Nothing speaks louder or more powerfully than a life of integrity.

Charles Swindoll

You should set the right kind of example for your friends . . . and vice-versa.

Criswell Freeman

A Father-Son Prayer

Dear Lord, help us follow in the footsteps of Your Son so that we can show other people what it really means to be a Christian. Amen

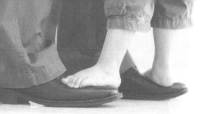

Devo 49

Obeying God

Be gentle with one another, sensitive. Forgive one another as quickly and thoroughly as God in Christ forgave you.

Ephesians 4:32 MSG

How hard is it to forgive people? Sometimes, it's very hard! But God tells us that we must forgive other people, even when we'd rather not forgive them. So, if you're angry with anybody (or if you're upset by something you yourself have done) it's time to forgive.

God instructs us to treat other people exactly as we wish to be treated. When we forgive others, we are obeying our Heavenly Father, and that's exactly what we must try to do.

A Timely Tip for Boys

Forgiving other people is not necessarily the same as forgetting. Yet even when you cannot forget the past, you should try not to focus on the past.

More from God's Word

See to it that no one repays evil for evil to anyone, but always pursue what is good for one another and for all.

1 Thessalonians 5:15 HCSB

A person's insight gives him patience, and his virtue is to overlook an offense.

Proverbs 19:11 HCSB

Be merciful, just as your Father also is merciful.

Luke 6:36 HCSB

A Timely Tip for Dads

Holding a grudge? Drop it! How can you expect your kids to forgive others if you don't? Never expect your children to be more forgiving than you are.

Some Very Bright Ideas

An eye for an eye and a tooth for a tooth . . . and pretty soon, everybody's blind and wearing dentures.

Anonymous

As you have received the mercy of God by the forgiveness of sin and the promise of eternal life, thus you must show mercy.

Billy Graham

Forgiveness is God's command.

Martin Luther

A Father-Son Prayer

Dear Lord, sometimes it's very hard to forgive those who have hurt us, but with Your help, we can do it. Today, help us forgive others, just as You have already forgiven us. Amen

Devo 50

Jesus Can Take Care of Our Problems

Do not love the world or the things that belong to the world. If anyone loves the world, love for the Father is not in him.

1 John 2:15 HCSB

An old hymn contains the words, "This world is not my home; I'm just passing through." Thank goodness! This crazy world can be a place of trouble and danger. Thankfully, your real home is heaven, a place where you can live forever with Jesus.

In John 16:33, Jesus tells us He has overcome the troubles of this world. We should trust Him, and we should obey His commandments. When we do, we are forever blessed by the Son of God and His Father in heaven.

A Timely Tip for Boys

If you pay attention to the world's messages, you're setting yourself up for trouble. If you pay attention to God's messages, you're setting yourself up for victory.

More from God's Word

Pure and undefiled religion before our God and Father is this: to look after orphans and widows in their distress and to keep oneself unstained by the world.

James 1:27 HCSB

Now we have not received the spirit of the world, but the Spirit who is from God, in order to know what has been freely given to us by God.

1 Corinthians 2:12 HCSB

No one should deceive himself. If anyone among you thinks he is wise in this age, he must become foolish so that he can become wise. For the wisdom of this world is foolishness with God, since it is written: He catches the wise in their craftiness.

1 Corinthians 3:18-19 HCSB

A Timely Tip for Dads

If you seek the things that God values, you will be satisfied; if you seek the things that the world values, you will be disappointed.

Some Very Bright Ideas

The Lord Jesus Christ is still praying for us. He wants us to be in the world but not of it.

Charles Stanley

If you give the devil an inch, he'll be a ruler.

Anonymous

Television has a way of attacking your senses and your heart. So be careful what you watch.

Criswell Freeman

A Father-Son Prayer

Dear Lord, we want to follow Your rules and follow Your Son. So today, instead of trying to impress other people, we'll try to please You. Amen

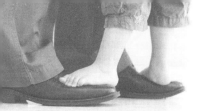

Everlasting Protection

The Lord is my rock, my fortress, and my deliverer, my God, my mountain where I seek refuge. My shield, the horn of my salvation, my stronghold, my refuge, and my Savior.

2 Samuel 22:2-3 HCSB

Life isn't always easy. Far from it! Sometimes, life can be very hard indeed. But even when we're upset or hurt, we must remember that we're protected by a loving Heavenly Father.

When we're worried, God can reassure us; when we're sad, God can comfort us. When our feelings are hurt, God is not just near, He is here. We must lift our thoughts and prayers to our Father in heaven. When we do, He will answer our prayers. Why? Because He is our Shepherd, and He has promised to protect us now and forever.

A Timely Tip for Boys

The best protection comes from the loving heart of God—and from the salvation that flows from His only begotten Son.

More from God's Word

Come near to God, and God will come near to you. You sinners, clean sin out of your lives. You who are trying to follow God and the world at the same time, make your thinking pure.

James 4:8 NCV

No, I will not abandon you as orphans—I will come to you.

John 14:18 NLT

Again, this is God's command: to believe in his personally named Son, Jesus Christ. He told us to love each other, in line with the original command. As we keep his commands, we live deeply and surely in him, and he lives in us. And this is how we experience his deep and abiding presence in us: by the Spirit he gave us.

1 John 3:23-24 MSG

A Timely Tip for Dads

He protects parents and children alike. So if you're feeling a little apprehensive about the future, fear not. God promises to protect every member of your family, and that includes you!

Some Very Bright Ideas

When you fall and skin your knees and skin your heart, He'll pick you up.

Charles Stanley

The Will of God will never take you where the Grace of God will not protect you.

Anonymous

God delights in spreading His protective wings and enfolding His frightened, weary, beaten-down, worn-out children.

Bill Hybels

A Father-Son Prayer

Dear Lord, because You watch over us, we don't have to be afraid. Because You are with us always, we can have hope. Thank You, Lord, for protecting us today, tomorrow, and forever. Amen

He Answers

For I know the thoughts that I think toward you, says the Lord, thoughts of peace and not of evil, to give you a future and a hope. Then you will call upon Me and go and pray to Me, and I will listen to you.

Jeremiah 29:11-12 NKJV

In case you've been wondering, wonder no more—God does answer your prayers. What God does not do is this: He does not always answer your prayers as soon as you might like, and He does not always answer your prayers by saying "Yes."

God answers prayers not only according to our wishes but also according to His master plan. And guess what? We don't know that plan . . . but we can know the Planner.

Are you praying? Then you can be sure that God is listening. And sometime soon, He'll answer!

A Timely Tip for Boys

Pray early and often. The more you talk to God, the more He will talk to you.

More from God's Word

And everything—whatever you ask in prayer, believing—you will receive.

Matthew 21:22 HCSB

Rejoice always! Pray constantly. Give thanks in everything, for this is God's will for you in Christ Jesus.

1 Thessalonians 5:16-18 HCSB

Therefore I want the men in every place to pray, lifting up holy hands without anger or argument.

1 Timothy 2:8 HCSB

A Timely Tip for Dads

Sometimes, the answer to prayer is "No." God doesn't grant all of our requests, nor should He. We must help our children understand that our prayers are answered by a sovereign, all-knowing God, and that we must trust His answers.

Some Very Bright Ideas

You don't need fancy words or religious phrases. Just tell God the way it really is.

Jim Cymbala

Prayer is never the least we can do; it is always the most!

A. W. Tozer

Faith in a prayer-hearing God will make a prayer-loving Christian.

Andrew Murray

A Father-Son Prayer

Dear Lord, You always hear our prayers. Remind us to pray often about the things we need and the things You want us to have. Amen

Devo 53

Nobody Likes 'Em

Therefore, if anyone is in Christ, he is a new creation; the old has gone, the new has come!

2 Corinthians 5:17 NIV

Mistakes: nobody likes 'em but everybody makes 'em. And you're no different! When you make mistakes (and you will), you should do your best to correct them, to learn from them, and pray for the wisdom to avoid those same mistakes in the future.

If you want to become smarter faster, you'll learn from your mistakes the first time you make them. When you do, that means that you won't keep making the same mistakes over and over again, and that's the smart way to live.

A Timely Tip for Boys

Made a mistake? Ask for forgiveness! If you've broken one of God's rules, you can always ask Him for His forgiveness. And He will always give it!

More from God's Word

If we confess our sins to him, he is faithful and just to forgive us and to cleanse us from every wrong.

1 John 1:9 NLT

Have mercy on me, O God, according to your unfailing love; according to your great compassion blot out my transgressions. Wash away all my iniquity and cleanse me from my sin.

Psalm 51:1-2 NIV

I will instruct you and teach you in the way you should go; I will counsel you and watch over you.

Psalm 32:8 NIV

A Timely Tip for Dads

When you fall short, ask for forgiveness. Nobody's perfect; no, not even you. When you make mistakes, as you most certainly will from time to time, ask for forgiveness, especially if you're seeking it from your kids. Your behavior will serve as a priceless example to your children.

Some Very Bright Ideas

Lord, when we are wrong, make us willing to change; and when we are right, make us easy to live with.

Peter Marshall

God is able to take mistakes, when they are committed to Him, and make of them something for our good and for His glory.

Ruth Bell Graham

We become a failure when we allow mistakes to take away our ability to learn, give, grow, and try again.

Susan Lenzkes

A Father-Son Prayer

Dear Lord, everybody makes mistakes, including us. When we make mistakes, help us learn from them. Let us use our mistakes, Father, to become better people and better Christians. Amen

The Blame Game

People's own foolishness ruins their lives, but in their minds they blame the Lord.

Proverbs 19:3 NCV

When something goes wrong, do you look for somebody to blame? And do you try to blame other people even if you're the one who made the mistake? Hopefully not!

It's silly to try to blame other people for your own mistakes, so don't do it.

If you've done something you're ashamed of, don't look for somebody to blame; look for a way to say, "I'm sorry, and I won't make that same mistake again."

A Timely Tip for Boys

It's very tempting to blame others when you make a mistake, but it's more honest to look in the mirror first.

More from God's Word

Get rid of all bitterness, rage, anger, harsh words, and slander, as well as all types of malicious behavior. Instead, be kind to each other, tenderhearted, forgiving one another, just as God through Christ has forgiven you.

Ephesians 4:31–32 NLT

Don't insist on getting even; that's not for you to do. "I'll do the judging," says God. "I'll take care of it."

Romans 12:19 MSG

See to it that no one repays evil for evil to anyone, but always pursue what is good for one another and for all.

1 Thessalonians 5:15 HCSB

A Timely Tip for Dads

If you take responsibility for your actions, you're headed in the right direction. If you try to blame others, you're headed down a dead-end street.

Some Very Bright Ideas

The single most important element in any human relationship is honesty—with oneself, with God, and with others.

Catherine Marshall

You'll never win the blame game, so why even bother to play?

Marie T. Freeman

Never use your problem as an excuse for bad attitudes or behavior.

Joyce Meyer

A Father-Son Prayer

Dear Lord, when we make mistakes, it's tempting to blame others. But blaming others is wrong. Help us accept responsibility, Father, for the mistakes we make. And help us learn from them. Amen

What Your Conscience Says About Forgiveness

Now the goal of our instruction is love from a pure heart, a good conscience, and a sincere faith.

1 Timothy 1:5 HCSB

God gave you something called a conscience: it's that little feeling that tells you whether something is right or wrong. Your conscience will usually tell you what to do and when to do it. Trust that feeling.

If you listen to your conscience, it won't be as hard for you to forgive people. Why? Because forgiving other people is the right thing to do. And, it's what God wants you to do. And it's what your conscience tells you to do. So what are you waiting for?

A Timely Tip for Boys

Trust the quiet inner voice of your conscience: Treat your conscience as you would a trusted advisor.

More from God's Word

So I strive always to keep my conscience clear before God and man.

Acts 24:16 NIV

If then you were raised with Christ, seek those things which are above, where Christ is, sitting at the right hand of God. Set your mind on things above, not on things on the earth.

Colossians 3:1-2 NKJV

Let us come near to God with a sincere heart and a sure faith, because we have been made free from a guilty conscience, and our bodies have been washed with pure water.

Hebrews 10:22 NCV

A Timely Tip for Dads

The more important the decision, the more carefully you should listen to your conscience.

Some Very Bright Ideas

If your conscience tells you to say no, then say it.

Criswell Freeman

Guilt is a gift that leads us to grace.

Franklin Graham

Your conscience is your alarm system. It's your protection.

Charles Stanley

Christian joy is a gift from God flowing from a good conscience.

St. Philip Neri

A Father-Son Prayer

Dear Lord, we know that we should forgive other people. So when it's time to forgive, that's exactly what we'll do. Amen

Positive Peer Pressure

My dear, dear friends, if God loved us like this, we certainly ought to love each other.

1 John 4:11 MSG

Are your friends the kind of kids who encourage you to behave yourself? If so, you've chosen your friends wisely.

But if your friends try to get you in trouble, perhaps it's time to think long and hard about making some new friends.

Whether you know it or not, you're probably going to behave like your friends behave. So pick out friends who make you want to behave better, not worse. When you do, you'll be saving yourself from a lot of trouble . . . a whole lot of trouble.

A Timely Tip for Boys

Choose wise friends, and listen carefully to the things they say.

More from God's Word

Do not be fooled: "Bad friends will ruin good habits."
1 Corinthians 15:33 NCV

My dear friend, do not follow what is bad; follow what is good.
3 John 1:11 NCV

Don't envy bad people; don't even want to be around them. All they think about is causing a disturbance; all they talk about is making trouble.

Proverbs 24:1-2 MSG

A Timely Tip for Dads

Do you want your son to choose well-behaved friends? If so, talk openly to your child about the wisdom of choosing friends who behave themselves.

Some Very Bright Ideas

God often keeps us on the path by guiding us through the counsel of friends and trusted spiritual advisors.

Bill Hybels

True friends will always lift you higher and challenge you to walk in a manner pleasing to our Lord.

Lisa Bevere

Do you want to be wise? Choose wise friends.

Charles Swindoll

A Father-Son Prayer

Dear Lord, the Bible teaches us to choose our friends carefully. And, that's what we intend to do every day of our lives. Amen

Devo 57

Be the Right Kind of Christian

The one who plants and the one who waters have the same purpose, and each will be rewarded for his own work.

1 Corinthians 3:8 NCV

Do you want to be the kind of Christian who God intends for you to be? It's up to you! You'll be the one who will decide how you behave.

If you decide to obey God and trust His Son, you will be rewarded now and forever. So guard your heart and trust your Heavenly Father. He will never lead you astray.

A Timely Tip for Boys

It's easy to blame others when you get into trouble . . . but it's wrong. Instead of trying to blame other people for your own misbehavior, take responsibility . . . and learn from your mistakes!

More from God's Word

But each person should examine his own work, and then he will have a reason for boasting in himself alone, and not in respect to someone else. For each person will have to carry his own load.

Galatians 6:4-5 HCSB

So then each of us shall give account of himself to God.

Romans 14:12 NKJV

"Therefore I will judge you, O house of Israel, every one according to his ways," says the Lord God.

Ezekiel 18:30 NKJV

A Timely Tip for Dads

It's easy to hold other people accountable, but real accountability begins with the man in the mirror. Think about one specific area of responsibility that is uniquely yours, and think about a specific step you can take today to better fulfill that responsibility.

Some Very Bright Ideas

You can't depend on anybody but the Lord and yourself, in that order.

Charlie Daniels

Action springs not from thought, but from a readiness for responsibility.

Dietrich Bonhoeffer

Although God causes all things to work together for good for His children, He still holds us accountable for our behavior.

Kay Arthur

A Father-Son Prayer

Dear Lord, thank You for watching over us. Help us understand what's right and do what's right, now and always. Amen

Peace at Home

My dear brothers, always be willing to listen and slow to speak. Do not become angry easily. Anger will not help you live a good life as God wants.

James 1:19 ICB

Sometimes, it's easy to become angry with the people we love most, and sometimes it's hard to forgive them. After all, we know that our family will still love us no matter how angry we become. But while it's easy to become angry at home, it's usually wrong.

The next time you're tempted to stay angry at a brother, or a sister, or a parent, remember that these are the people who love you more than anybody else! Then, calm down, and forgive them . . . NOW! Because peace is always beautiful, especially when it's peace at your house.

A Timely Tip for Boys

If you're mad at someone, don't say the first thing that comes to your mind and don't strike out in anger. Instead, catch your breath and start counting until you are once again in control of your temper. If you get to a million and you're still counting, go to bed! You'll feel better in the morning.

More from God's Word

All bitterness, anger and wrath, insult and slander must be removed from you, along with all wickedness. And be kind and compassionate to one another, forgiving one another, just as God also forgave you in Christ.

Ephesians 4:31-32 HCSB

A gentle answer turns away anger, but a harsh word stirs up wrath.

Proverbs 15:1 HCSB

But now you must also put away all the following: anger, wrath, malice, slander, and filthy language from your mouth.

Colossians 3:8 HCSB

A Timely Tip for Dads

The way that you manage your own anger will speak volumes to your children. If you can control your anger, you'll help them see the wisdom in controlling theirs.

Some Very Bright Ideas

When you strike out in anger, you may miss the other person, but you will always hit yourself.

Jim Gallery

When you lose your temper . . . you lose.

Criswell Freeman

Bitterness and anger, usually over trivial things, make havoc of homes, churches, and friendships.

Warren Wiersbe

A Father-Son Prayer

Dear Lord, if we become angry with family or friends, calm us down. Jesus forgave everybody, even the people who hurt Him. We should, too. Amen

Devo 59

The Right Choice

But Daniel purposed in his heart that he would not defile himself....

Daniel 1:8 KJV

Your life is a series of choices. From the instant you wake up in the morning until the moment you nod off to sleep at night, you make lots of decisions: decisions about the things you do, decisions about the words you speak, and decisions about the thoughts you choose to think.

So, if you want to lead a life that is pleasing to God, you must make choices that are pleasing to Him. He deserves no less . . . and neither, for that matter, do you.

A Timely Tip for Boys

When you make wise choices, you make everybody happy. You make your parents happy, you make your teachers happy, you make your friends happy, and you make God happy!

More from God's Word

The thing you should want most is God's kingdom and doing what God wants. Then all these other things you need will be given to you.

Matthew 6:33 NCV

If you don't know what you're doing, pray to the Father. He loves to help. You'll get his help, and won't be condescended to when you ask for it. Ask boldly, believingly, without a second thought. People who "worry their prayers" are like wind-whipped waves. Don't think you're going to get anything from the Master that way, adrift at sea, keeping all your options open.

James 1:5-8 MSG

The one who lives with integrity lives securely, but whoever perverts his ways will be found out.

Proverbs 10:9 HCSB

A Timely Tip for Dads

Live according to the principles you teach. The sermons you live are far more important than the sermons you preach.

Some Very Bright Ideas

Every moment of resistance to temptation is a victory.

Frederick William Faber

Every day of our lives we make choices about how we're going to live that day.

Luci Swindoll

To refuse to respond is in itself a response.

Madeleine L'Engle

A Father-Son Prayer

Dear Lord, we want to follow Jesus this day and every day. Help us to become more like Him, and help us to share His message with our family and friends. Amen

Be Happy Today

But happy are those . . . whose hope is in the LORD their God.

Psalm 146:5 NLT

If we could decide to be happy "once and for all," life would be so much simpler, but it doesn't seem to work that way. If we want happiness to last, we need to create good thoughts every day that we live. Yesterday's good thoughts don't count . . . we've got to think more good thoughts now.

Each new day is a gift from God, so treat it that way. Think about it like this: today is another wonderful chance to celebrate God's gifts.

So celebrate—starting now—and keep celebrating forever!

A Timely Tip for Boys

Better self-control can help make you happy: the better you behave, the more fun you'll have. And don't let anybody try to tell you otherwise.

More from God's Word

But the truly happy person is the one who carefully studies God's perfect law that makes people free. He continues to study it. He listens to God's teaching and does not forget what he heard. Then he obeys what God's teaching says. When he does this, it makes him happy.

James 1:25 ICB

Happy are those who fear the Lord. Yes, happy are those who delight in doing what he commands.

Psalm 112:1 NLT

Delight thyself also in the LORD; and he shall give thee the desires of thine heart.

Psalm 37:4 KJV

A Timely Tip for Dads

The best day to be happy is this one. Don't spend your whole life in the waiting room. Make up your mind to celebrate today.

Some Very Bright Ideas

The secret of a happy life is to do your duty and trust in God.

Sam Jones

Learning how to forgive and forget is one of the secrets of a happy Christian life.

Warren Wiersbe

Whoever possesses God is happy.

St. Augustine

A Father-Son Prayer

Dear Lord, we have so many reasons to be happy. Let us think good thoughts and look for the good in other people. And, help us to be joyful Christians today and always. Amen

Devo 61

An Honest Heart

In every way be an example of doing good deeds. When you teach, do it with honesty and seriousness.

Titus 2:7 NCV

Where does honesty begin? In your own heart and your own head. If you sincerely want to be an honest person, then you must ask God to help you find the courage and the determination to be honest all of the time.

Honesty is not a "sometimes" thing. If you intend to be a truthful person, you must make truthfulness a habit that becomes so much a part of you that you don't have to decide whether or not you're going to tell the truth. Instead, you will simply tell the truth because it's the kind of person you are.

Lying is an easy habit to fall into, and a terrible one. So make up your mind that you're going to be an honest person, and then stick to your decision. That's what your parents want you to do, and that's what God wants, too. And since they love you more than you know, trust them. And always tell the truth.

A Timely Tip for Boys

Little white lies? Beware! You may think that there's a big difference between "little" lies and king-sized ones. Unfortunately, little white lies have a tendency to grow into big trouble . . . in a hurry.

More from God's Word

For there is nothing covered, that shall not be revealed; neither hid, that shall not be known. Therefore, whatsoever ye have spoken in darkness shall be heard in the light; and that which ye have spoken in the ear in closets shall be proclaimed upon the housetops.

Luke 12:2-3 KJV

Ye shall not steal, neither deal falsely, neither lie one to another.

Leviticus 19:11 KJV

A Timely Tip for Dads

If your son tells a falsehood, talk about it. Even "little white lies" are worthy of a parent-to-child talk; the bigger the lie, the bigger the talk.

Some Very Bright Ideas

God doesn't expect you to be perfect, but he does insist on complete honesty.

Rick Warren

One thing that is important for stable emotional health is honesty—with self and with others.

Joyce Meyer

Those who are given to white lies soon become color blind.

Anonymous

A Father-Son Prayer

Dear Lord, we know that it's good to be honest. So please help us form the habit of being honest with everybody, even when it's hard. Amen

Your Picture

For God so loved the world that he gave his only Son, so that everyone who believes in him will not perish but have eternal life.

John 3:16 NLT

If God had a refrigerator in heaven, your picture would be on it! And that fact should make you feel very good about the person you are and the person you can become.

God's love for you is bigger and more wonderful than you can imagine. So do this, and do it right now: accept God's love with open arms and welcome His Son Jesus into your heart. When you do, you'll feel better about yourself . . . and your life will be changed forever.

A Timely Tip for Boys

Remember: God's love for you is too big to understand with your brain . . . but it's not too big to feel with your heart.

More from God's Word

For the LORD your God has arrived to live among you. He is a mighty savior. He will rejoice over you with great gladness. With his love, he will calm all your fears. He will exult over you by singing a happy song.

Zephaniah 3:17 NLT

But God demonstrates His own love toward us, in that while we were still sinners, Christ died for us.

Romans 5:8 NKJV

For he chose us in him before the creation of the world to be holy and blameless in his sight. In love he predestined us to be adopted as his sons through Jesus Christ, in accordance with his pleasure and will....

Ephesians 1:4-5 NIV

A Timely Tip for Dads

Remember that God's love doesn't simply flow to your children; it flows to you, too. And because God loves you, you can be certain that you, like your child, are wonderfully made and amazingly blessed.

Some Very Bright Ideas

We must pray not first of all because it feels good or helps, but because God loves us and wants our attention.

Henri Nouwen

Because we are rooted and grounded in love, we can be relaxed and at ease, knowing that our acceptance is not based on our performance or our perfect behavior.

Joyce Meyer

From the outset, John makes it clear that our love is not an originating love but a responding love. "We love because he first loved us" (1 John 4:19).

Richard Foster

A Father-Son Prayer

Dear God, we know that Your love lasts forever. We thank You, Father, for Your amazing love. Every day, we will share Your love with others, and we will do our best to walk in the footsteps of Your Son. Amen

He Is Everywhere

God did this so that men would seek him and perhaps reach out for him and find him, though he is not far from each one of us.
Acts 17:27 NIV

God is everywhere you have ever been. And He is everywhere you will ever go. That's why you can speak to God any time you need to.

If you are afraid or discouraged, you can turn to God for strength. If you are worried, you can trust God's promises. And if you are happy, you can thank Him for His gifts.

God is right here, and so are you. And He's waiting patiently to hear from you, so why not have a word with Him right now?

A Timely Tip for Boys

If you're here, God is here. If you're there, God is, too. You can't get away from Him or His love . . . thank goodness!

More from God's Word

No, I will not abandon you as orphans—I will come to you.

John 14:18 NLT

Again, this is God's command: to believe in his personally named Son, Jesus Christ. He told us to love each other, in line with the original command. As we keep his commands, we live deeply and surely in him, and he lives in us. And this is how we experience his deep and abiding presence in us: by the Spirit he gave us.

1 John 3:23-24 MSG

You will seek Me and find Me when you search for Me with all your heart.

Jeremiah 29:13 HCSB

A Timely Tip for Dads

God isn't far away. He's right here, right now. And He wants to hear from you now.

Some Very Bright Ideas

God is in the midst of whatever has happened, is happening, and will happen.

Charles Swindoll

Get yourself into the presence of the loving Father. Just place yourself before Him, and look up into, His face; think of His love, His wonderful, tender, pitying love.

Andrew Murray

Because He is spirit, He fills heaven and earth.

Arthur W. Pink

A Father-Son Prayer

Dear Lord, You are always with us, and You are always listening to our thoughts and to our prayers. We will pray to You often, and we will trust in You always. Amen

Draw a Picture Together about God's Love

Devo 64

Each Day Is a Gift

How happy are those who can live in your house, always singing your praises. How happy are those who are strong in the Lord....

Psalm 84:4-5 NLT

God wants you to have a happy, joyful life. But that doesn't mean that you'll be happy all the time. Sometimes, you won't feel happy, and when you aren't, your attitude won't be very good.

When you're feeling a little tired or sad, here's something to remember: This day is a gift from God. And it's up to you to enjoy this day by trying to be cheerful, helpful, courteous, and well behaved. How can you do these things? A good place to start is by doing your best to think good thoughts.

A Timely Tip for Boys

To make happiness last, we must obey God while celebrating His blessings. To make happiness disappear, we need only disobey God while ignoring His blessings.

More from God's Word

A joyful heart is good medicine, but a broken spirit dries up the bones.

Proverbs 17:22 HCSB

How happy is the man who does not follow the advice of the wicked, or take the path of sinners, or join a group of mockers!

Psalm 1:1 HCSB

How happy are those whose way is blameless, who live according to the law of the Lord! Happy are those who keep His decrees and seek Him with all their heart.

Psalm 119:1-2 HCSB

A Timely Tip for Dads

Your children deserve to grow up in a happy home. As a parent, you owe it to them (and to yourself) to provide that kind of home.

Some Very Bright Ideas

Our thoughts, not our circumstances, determine our happiness.

John Maxwell

I am truly happy with Jesus Christ. I couldn't live without Him.

Ruth Bell Graham

There is no correlation between wealth and happiness.

Larry Burkett

A Father-Son Prayer

Dear Lord, You have given us more blessings than we can count. We will do our best to be joyful Christians as we give thanks for Your blessings, for Your love, and for Your Son. Amen

Devo 65

His Joy, Our Joy

I've told you these things for a purpose: that my joy might be your joy, and your joy wholly mature.

John 15:11 MSG

Christ made it clear to His followers: He intended that His joy would become their joy. And it's still true today: Christ intends that His believers share His love with His joy in their hearts. Yet sometimes, amid the inevitable hustle and bustle of life, we can lose—at least for a while—the joy of Christ as we wrestle with the challenges of daily living.

C. H. Spurgeon, the 19th-century English clergyman, advised, "The Lord is glad to open the gate to every knocking soul. It opens very freely. Have faith and enter at this moment through holy courage. If you knock with a heavy heart, you shall yet sing with joy of spirit. Never be discouraged!" How true!

A Timely Tip for Boys

Joy does not depend upon your circumstances, but on your relationship with God.

More from God's Word

Rejoice in the Lord always. I will say it again: Rejoice!

Philippians 4:4 HCSB

Make me to hear joy and gladness.

Psalm 51:8 KJV

Now I am coming to You, and I speak these things in the world so that they may have My joy completed in them.

John 17:13 HCSB

Sing a new song to him; play well and joyfully.

Psalm 33:3 NCV

A Timely Tip for Dads

If you want to teach your child what it means to be a joyful Christian . . . be one.

Some Very Bright Ideas

Joy is not the same as happiness—although they may overlap. Happiness depends on circumstances; joy depends on God.

Billy Graham

God is real, His promises are true, time on earth is an exciting adventure, and heaven is my home. Without question it has been a joyous journey.

Bill Bright

When Jesus Christ is the source of our joy, no words can describe it.

Billy Graham

A Father-Son Prayer

Dear Lord, You have given us so many blessings, starting with our family. We will keep joy in our heart as we thank You, Lord, for every single blessing You've given us. Amen

Start Sharing Now

Never walk away from someone who deserves help; your hand is God's hand for that person.

Proverbs 3:27 MSG

When is the best time to share? Whenever you can—and that means right now, if possible. When you start thinking about the things you can share, you probably think mostly about things that belong to you (like toys or clothes), but there are many more things you can share (like love, kindness, encouragement, and prayers). That means you have the opportunity to share something with somebody almost any time you want. And that's exactly what God wants you to do—so start sharing now and don't ever stop.

A Timely Tip for Boys

What does the Bible say about sharing our possessions? The Bible answers this question very clearly: when other people need our help, we should gladly share the things we have.

More from God's Word

In every way I've shown you that by laboring like this, it is necessary to help the weak and to keep in mind the words of the Lord Jesus, for He said, "It is more blessed to give than to receive."

Acts 20:35 HCSB

Instruct those who are rich in the present age not to be arrogant or to set their hope on the uncertainty of wealth, but on God, who richly provides us with all things to enjoy. Instruct them to do good, to be rich in good works, to be generous, willing to share.

1 Timothy 6:17-18 HCSB

The one who blesses others is abundantly blessed; those who help others are helped.

Proverbs 11:25 MSG

A Timely Tip for Dads

Your children will learn how to treat others by watching you (not by listening to you!). Your acts of kindness and generosity will speak far louder than words.

Some Very Bright Ideas

It is the duty of every Christian to be Christ to his neighbor.

Martin Luther

He climbs highest who helps another up.

Zig Ziglar

The #1 rule of friendship is the Golden one.

Jim Gallery

A Father-Son Prayer

Dear Lord, there are so many things that we can share. Help us never to forget the importance of sharing our possessions, our prayers, and our love with family members and friends. Amen

Your Family Has Rules

This is how we are sure that we have come to know Him: by keeping His commands.

1 John 2:3 HCSB

Face facts: your family has rules that you're not supposed to break. You're old enough to know right from wrong, so you're old enough to do something about it. In other words, you should always try to obey your family's rules.

How can you tell "the right thing" from "the wrong thing"? By listening carefully to your parents, that's how.

The more self-control you have, the easier it is to obey your parents. Why? Because, when you learn to think first and do things next, you avoid making silly mistakes. So here's what you should do: First, slow down long enough to listen to your parents. Then, do the things that you know your parents want you to do.

Face facts: your family has rules . . . and it's better for everybody when you obey them.

A Timely Tip for Boys

Since you love your family, show it by behaving yourself and obeying your family's rules!

More from God's Word

Therefore, get your minds ready for action, being self-disciplined, and set your hope completely on the grace to be brought to you at the revelation of Jesus Christ. As obedient children, do not be conformed to the desires of your former ignorance but, as the One who called you is holy, you also are to be holy in all your conduct.

1 Peter 1:13-15 HCSB

Who is wise and understanding among you? He should show his works by good conduct with wisdom's gentleness.

James 3:13 HCSB

You must follow the Lord your God and fear Him. You must keep His commands and listen to His voice; you must worship Him and remain faithful to Him.

Deuteronomy 13:4 HCSB

A Timely Tip for Dads

Obedience begins at home. If your children don't learn obedience between the four walls of your home, they probably won't learn it anywhere else.

Some Very Bright Ideas

You may not always see immediate results, but all God wants is your obedience and faithfulness.

Vonette Bright

The ultimate response to Jesus' teaching is belief and obedience.

John MacArthur

Obedience is the outward expression of your love of God.

Henry Blackaby

A Father-Son Prayer

Dear Lord, we know that You have rules, and we know that it's important to obey those rules. Help us to follow in the footsteps of Your Son, today and every day.

Jesus Offers Peace

I have told you these things, so that in me you may have peace. In this world you will have trouble. But take heart! I have overcome the world.

John 16:33 NIV

Jesus offers us peace . . . peace in our hearts and peace in our homes. But He doesn't force us to enjoy His peace—we can either accept His peace or not.

When we accept the peace of Jesus Christ by opening up our hearts to Him, we feel much better about ourselves, our families, and our lives.

Would you like to feel a little better about yourself and a little better about your corner of the world? Then open up your heart to Jesus, because that's where real peace begins.

A Timely Tip for Boys

You have a big role to play in helping to maintain a peaceful home. It's a big job, so don't be afraid to ask for help . . . especially God's help.

More from God's Word

The result of righteousness will be peace; the effect of righteousness will be quiet confidence forever.

Isaiah 32:17 HCSB

Peace, peace to you, and peace to him who helps you, for your God helps you.

1 Chronicles 12:18 HCSB

Grace, mercy, and peace will be with us from God the Father and from Jesus Christ, the Son of the Father, in truth and love.

2 John 1:3 HCSB

A Timely Tip for Dads

Peace begins at home. As the parent, you're in charge of keeping the peace and sharing it. It's a big job, so don't be afraid to ask for help . . . especially God's help.

Some Very Bright Ideas

No Jesus, no peace; Know Jesus, know peace!

Anonymous

Christ alone can bring lasting peace—peace with God—peace among men and nations—and peace within our hearts.

Billy Graham

God cannot give us happiness and peace apart from Himself, because it is not there. There is no such thing.

C. S. Lewis

In the center of a hurricane there is absolute quiet and peace. There is no safer place than in the center of the will of God.

Corrie ten Boom

A Father-Son Prayer

Dear Lord, You know our hearts. Help us to say things, to do things, and to think things that are pleasing to You. Amen

What's Really Important

A pretentious, showy life is an empty life; a plain and simple life is a full life.

Proverbs 13:7 MSG

"**S**o much stuff to shop for, and so little time . . ." These words describe lots of people, but please don't let those words describe you!

The Bible teaches this important lesson: it's not good to be too concerned about money or the stuff that money can buy. So don't worry too much about the things you can buy in stores. Worry more about obeying your parents and obeying your Heavenly Father—that's what's really important.

A Timely Tip for Boys

The world says, "Buy more stuff." God says, "Stuff isn't important." Believe God.

More from God's Word

Don't collect for yourselves treasures on earth, where moth and rust destroy and where thieves break in and steal. But collect for yourselves treasures in heaven, where neither moth nor rust destroys, and where thieves don't break in and steal. For where your treasure is, there your heart will be also.

Matthew 6:19-21 HCSB

No one can serve two masters; for either he will hate the one and love the other, or else he will be loyal to the one and despise the other. You cannot serve God and mammon.

Matthew 6:24 NKJV

And He said to them, "Take heed and beware of covetousness, for one's life does not consist in the abundance of the things he possesses."

Luke 12:15 NKJV

A Timely Tip for Dads

Everything we have is on loan from God. Remember that your real riches are in heaven, so conduct yourself accordingly . . . and teach your children to do likewise.

Some Very Bright Ideas

Our ultimate aim in life is not to be healthy, wealthy, prosperous, or problem free. Our ultimate aim in life is to bring glory to God.

Anne Graham Lotz

If you want to be truly happy, you won't find it on an endless quest for more stuff. You'll find it in receiving God's generosity and in passing that generosity along.

Bill Hybels

No one is truly happy if he has what he wants, but only if he wants something he should have.

St. Augustine

A Father-Son Prayer

Dear God, help us remember that the stuff we own isn't very important. What's really important is the love that we feel in our hearts for our family, the love that we feel for Jesus, and the love that we feel for You. Amen

A Cheerful Heart

Jacob said, "For what a relief it is to see your friendly smile. It is like seeing the smile of God!"

Genesis 33:10 NLT

The Bible tells us that a cheerful heart is like medicine: it makes us feel better. Where does cheerfulness begin? It begins inside each of us; it begins in the heart. So let's be thankful to God for His blessings, and let's show our thanks by sharing good cheer wherever we go.

So, make sure that you share a smile and a kind word with as many people as you can. This old world needs all the cheering up it can get . . . and so do your friends.

A Timely Tip for Boys

If you need a little cheering up, find somebody else who needs cheering up, too. Then, do your best to brighten that person's day. When you do, you'll discover that cheering up other people is a wonderful way to cheer yourself up, too!

More from God's Word

Bright eyes cheer the heart; good news strengthens the bones.
Proverbs 15:30 HCSB

A cheerful heart has a continual feast.
Proverbs 15:15 HCSB

Is anyone cheerful? He should sing praises.
James 5:13 HCSB

A cheerful heart is good medicine, but a crushed spirit dries up the bones.
Proverbs 17:22 NIV

A Timely Tip for Dads

Cheerfulness is contagious. Remember that a cheerful family starts with cheerful parents.

Some Very Bright Ideas

Hope is the power of being cheerful in circumstances which we know to be desperate.

G. K. Chesterton

The people whom I have seen succeed best in life have always been cheerful and hopeful people who went about their business with a smile on their faces.

Charles Kingsley

God is good, and heaven is forever. And if those two facts don't cheer you up, nothing will.

Marie T. Freeman

A Father-Son Prayer

Dear Lord, let us count our blessings and be thankful. And help us remember not to whine about the things we don't have. Amen

Devo 71

Stop and Think

Now you must rid yourselves of all such things as these: anger, rage, malice....

Colossians 3:8 NIV

When we lose control of our emotions, we do things that we shouldn't do. Sometimes, we throw tantrums. How silly! Other times we pout or whine. Too bad!

The Bible tells us that it is foolish to become angry and that it is wise to remain calm. That's why we should learn to slow down and think about things before we do them.

Do you want to make life better for yourself and for your family? Then be patient and think things through. Stop and think before you do things, not after. It's the wise thing to do.

A Timely Tip for Boys

If you're a little angry, think carefully before you speak. If you're very angry, think very carefully. Otherwise, you might say something in anger that you regret later.

More from God's Word

Don't let your spirit rush to be angry, for anger abides in the heart of fools.

Ecclesiastes 7:9 HCSB

My dearly loved brothers, understand this: everyone must be quick to hear, slow to speak, and slow to anger, for man's anger does not accomplish God's righteousness.

James 1:19-20 HCSB

A fool's displeasure is known at once, but whoever ignores an insult is sensible.

Proverbs 12:16 HCSB

A Timely Tip for Dads

When your child becomes upset, you'll be tempted to become upset, too. Resist that temptation. Remember that in a house filled with kids and grownups, you're the grown-up. And it's up to you to remain calm even when other, less mature members of the family can't.

Some Very Bright Ideas

If your temper gets the best of you . . . then other people get
to see the worst in you.

Criswell Freeman

Doomed are the hotheads! Unhappy are they who lose their
cool and are too proud to say, "I'm sorry."

Robert Schuller

No one can heal himself by wounding someone else.

St. Ambrose

A Father-Son Prayer

*Dear Lord, You know that we can be impatient at times. And
sometimes, we become angry. When we become upset, please
calm us down, Lord, and help us forgive the people who have
made us angry. We know that Jesus forgave other people, and we
should, too. Amen*

God Wrote a Book

For I am not ashamed of the gospel, because it is God's power for salvation to everyone who believes.

Romans 1:16 HCSB

If you want to know God, you should read the book He wrote. It's called the Bible (of course!), and God uses it to teach you and guide you. The Bible is not like any other book. It is an amazing gift from your Heavenly Father.

D. L. Moody observed, "The Bible was not given to increase our knowledge but to change our lives." God's Holy Word is, indeed, a life-changing, one-of-a-kind treasure. Handle it with care, but more importantly, handle it every day!

A Timely Tip for Boys

Start learning about Jesus, and keep learning about Him as long as you live. His story never grows old, and His teachings never fail.

More from God's Word

Your word is a lamp for my feet and a light on my path.
Psalm 119:105 HCSB

Heaven and earth will pass away, but My words will never pass away.
Matthew 24:35 HCSB

All Scripture is inspired by God and is profitable for teaching, for rebuking, for correcting, for training in righteousness, so that the man of God may be complete, equipped for every good work.
2 Timothy 3:16-17 HCSB

A Timely Tip for Dads

Read your Bible every morning. When you start each day by studying God's Word, you'll change the quality and direction of your life.

Some Very Bright Ideas

I believe the Bible is the best gift God has ever given to men. All the good from the Savior of the world is communicated to us through this book.

Abraham Lincoln

I study the Bible as I gather apples. First, I shake the whole tree that the ripest might fall. Then I shake each limb; I shake each branch and every twig. Then, I look under every leaf.

Martin Luther

The devil is not afraid of a Bible that has dust on it.

Anonymous

A Father-Son Prayer

Dear Lord, we thank You for Your Son. Jesus is the best friend our world has ever known. And, Jesus is our friend and Savior, too. So, we will study Your Word, Lord, and follow in the footsteps of Your Son, now and always. Amen

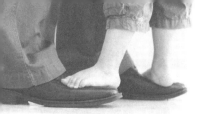

Self-Control and Patience

All athletes practice strict self-control. They do it to win a prize that will fade away, but we do it for an eternal prize.

1 Corinthians 9:25 NLT

The Book of Proverbs tells us that self-control and patience are very good things to have. But for most of us, self-control and patience can also be very hard things to learn.

Are you having trouble being patient? And are you having trouble slowing down long enough to think before you act? If so, remember that self-control takes practice, and lots of it, so keep trying. And if you make a mistake, don't be too upset. After all, if you're going to be a really patient person, you shouldn't just be patient with others; you should also be patient with yourself.

A Timely Tip for Boys

Sometimes, the best way to control yourself is to slow yourself down. Then, you can think about the things you're about to do before you do them.

More from God's Word

So prepare your minds for service and have self-control.

1 Peter 1:13 NCV

Discipline yourself for the purpose of godliness.

1 Timothy 4:7 NASB

So don't lose a minute in building on what you've been given, complementing your basic faith with good character, spiritual understanding, alert discipline, passionate patience, reverent wonder, warm friendliness, and generous love, each dimension fitting into and developing the others.

2 Peter 1:5-7 MSG

A Timely Tip for Dads

If you expect your son to have self-control, then you must have it, too. When it comes to parenting, you can't really teach it if you won't really live it.

Some Very Bright Ideas

Your thoughts are the determining factor as to whose mold you are conformed to. Control your thoughts and you control the direction of your life.

Charles Stanley

We are so used to living in an instant world that it is difficult to wait for anything.

Kay Arthur

Patience pays. Impatience costs.

Criswell Freeman

A Father-Son Prayer

Dear Lord, today and every day, we ask that You help us slow down and think about things before we do them. And, when we slow down to think about things, help us discover ways to follow in the footsteps of Your Son. Amen

Devo 74

Letting Other People Know What It Means to Be a Christian

But respect Christ as the holy Lord in your hearts. Always be ready to answer everyone who asks you to explain about the hope you have.

1 Peter 3:15 NCV

Every Christian, each in his or her own way, has a responsibility to share the Good News of Jesus. And it's important to remember that we bear testimony through both words and actions. Wise Christians follow the advice of St. Francis of Assisi who advised, "Preach the gospel at all times and, if necessary, use words."

As you think about how your example influences others, remember that actions speak louder than words . . . much louder!

A Timely Tip for Boys

Remember this: You share your testimony through words and actions. And the actions speak louder.

More from God's Word

You are the light of the world. A city that is set on a hill cannot be hidden. Nor do they light a lamp and put it under a basket, but on a lampstand, and it gives light to all who are in the house. Let your light so shine before men, that they may see your good works and glorify your Father in heaven.

Matthew 5:14–16 NKJV

Whatever I tell you in the dark, speak in the light; and what you hear in the ear, preach on the housetops.

Matthew 10:27 NKJV

And I say to you, anyone who acknowledges Me before men, the Son of Man will also acknowledge him before the angels of God; but whoever denies Me before men will be denied before the angels of God.

Luke 12:8-9 HCSB

A Timely Tip for Dads

Have you made the decision to allow Christ to reign over your heart? If so, you have an important story to tell: yours.

Some Very Bright Ideas

Our faith grows by expression. If we want to keep our faith, we must share it. We must act.

Billy Graham

When you don't witness, you just did.

Anonymous

Being an effective witness means that we call attention to our testimony and leave the results to Him.

Calvin Miller

A Father-Son Prayer

Dear Lord, today and every day, let us share the Good News of Your Son Jesus. And, let the lives that we live and the words that we speak bear testimony to our faith in Him. Amen

When We're Worried

Give all your worries and cares to God, for he cares about what happens to you.

1 Peter 5:6 NLT

When we're worried, there are two places we should take our concerns: to the people who love and care for us and to God.

When troubles arise, it helps to talk about them with parents, grandparents, and concerned adults. But we shouldn't stop there: we should also talk to God through our prayers.

If you're worried about something, you can pray about it any time you want. And remember that God is always listening, and He always wants to hear from you.

So when you're worried, try this plan: talk and pray. Talk to the grown-ups who love you, and pray to the Heavenly Father who made you. The more you talk and the more you pray, the better you'll feel.

A Timely Tip for Boys

Troubles will pass more quickly if you spend more time solving problems and less time fretting over them.

More from God's Word

Don't worry about anything, but in everything, through prayer and petition with thanksgiving, let your requests be made known to God.

Philippians 4:6 HCSB

Therefore don't worry about tomorrow, because tomorrow will worry about itself. Each day has enough trouble of its own.

Matthew 6:34 HCSB

Yea, though I walk through the valley of the shadow of death, I will fear no evil: for thou art with me; thy rod and thy staff they comfort me.

Psalm 23:4 KJV

A Timely Tip for Dads

If you're worried about your future, your family, or anything else, for that matter, pray about it. God is bigger than your problems.

Some Very Bright Ideas

Claim all of God's promises in the Bible. Your sins, your worries, your life—you may cast them all on Him.

Corrie ten Boom

God may say "Wait," but He never says, "Worry."

Anonymous

God is bigger than your problems. Whatever worries press upon you today, put them in God's hands and leave them there.

Billy Graham

A Father-Son Prayer

Dear Lord, when we are discouraged or afraid, we can always talk to You. We thank You for Your love, Father . . . and we thank You for our family. Amen

Every Day Is a Special Day

David and the whole house of Israel were celebrating before the Lord.

2 Samuel 6:5 HCSB

Every day should be a time for celebration, and hopefully, you feel like celebrating! After all, this day (like every other day) gives you the chance to thank God for all the wonderful things He has given you.

So don't wait for birthdays or holidays—make every day a special day, including this one. Take time to pause and thank God for His gifts. He deserves your thanks, and you deserve to celebrate!

A Timely Tip for Boys

If you don't feel like celebrating, start counting your blessings. Before long, you'll realize that you have plenty of reasons to celebrate.

More from God's Word

This is the day the LORD has made; we will rejoice and be glad in it.

Psalm 118:24 NKJV

A joyful heart is good medicine, but a broken spirit dries up the bones.

Proverbs 17:22 HCSB

How happy is the man who does not follow the advice of the wicked, or take the path of sinners, or join a group of mockers!

Psalm 1:1 HCSB

A Timely Tip for Dads

Every day should be a cause for celebration. By celebrating the gift of life, you protect your heart from the dangers of pessimism, regret, hopelessness, and bitterness.

Some Very Bright Ideas

Live in the present and make the most of your opportunities to enjoy your family and friends.

Barbara Johnson

Joy is the direct result of having God's perspective on our daily lives and the effect of loving our Lord enough to obey His commands and trust His promises.

Bill Bright

Our sense of joy, satisfaction, and fulfillment in life increases, no matter what the circumstances, if we are in the center of God's will.

Billy Graham

A Father-Son Prayer

Dear Lord, help us remember that every day is a cause for celebration. Today, we will keep joy in our hearts as we celebrate Your blessings and Your Son. Amen

That Little Voice

For God is pleased with you when, for the sake of your conscience, you patiently endure unfair treatment.

1 Peter 2:19 NLT

When you know that you're doing what's right, you'll feel better about yourself. Why? Because you have a little voice in your head called your "conscience." Your conscience is a feeling that tells you whether something is right or wrong—and it's what makes you feel better about yourself when you know you've done the right thing.

Your conscience is an important tool. Pay attention to it! The more you listen to your conscience, the easier it is to behave yourself. So here's great advice: first, slow down long enough to figure out the right thing to do—and then do it! When you do, you'll be proud of yourself . . . and other people will be proud of you, too.

A Timely Tip for Boys

That tiny little voice inside your head is called your conscience. Treat it like a trusted friend: Listen to the things it says; it's usually right!

More from God's Word

Now the goal of our instruction is love from a pure heart, a good conscience, and a sincere faith.

1 Timothy 1:5 HCSB

I always do my best to have a clear conscience toward God and men.

Acts 24:16 HCSB

Let us draw near with a true heart in full assurance of faith, our hearts sprinkled clean from an evil conscience and our bodies washed in pure water.

Hebrews 10:22 HCSB

A Timely Tip for Dads

Sometimes, the little voice that we hear in our heads can be the echoes of our own parents' voices. Now that you're a parent, you're the one whose words will echo down through the hearts and minds of future generations. It's a big responsibility, but with God's help, you're up to the challenge.

Some Very Bright Ideas

Every secret act of character, conviction, and courage has been observed in living color by our omniscient God.

Bill Hybels

Your conscience is your alarm system. It's your protection.

Charles Stanley

God gave you a conscience for one reason—to use it.

Criswell Freeman

A Father-Son Prayer

Dear Lord, You have given us a conscience that tells us what is right and what is wrong. We will listen to that quiet voice, Father, so we can do the right thing today and every day. Amen

When Things Go Wrong

But as for you, be strong; don't be discouraged, for your work has a reward.

2 Chronicles 15:7 HCSB

Face facts: some days are more wonderful than other days. Sometimes, everything seems to go right, and on other days, many things seem to go wrong. But here's something to remember: even when you're disappointed with the way things turn out, God is near . . . and He loves you very much!

If you're disappointed, worried, sad, or afraid, you can talk to your parents and to God. And you will certainly feel better when you do!

A Timely Tip for Boys

Things didn't work out? When you're disappointed about something, you can always talk to your parents . . . and you should!

More from God's Word

We take the good days from God—why not also the bad days?

Job 2:10 MSG

We are hard pressed on every side, yet not crushed; we are perplexed, but not in despair.

2 Corinthians 4:8 NKJV

Whatever has been born of God conquers the world. This is the victory that has conquered the world: our faith.

1 John 5:4 HCSB

A Timely Tip for Dads

Don't spend too much time asking, "Why me, Lord?" Instead, ask, "What now, Lord?" and then get to work. When you do, you'll feel much better.

Some Very Bright Ideas

Often God has to shut a door in our face so that he can subsequently open the door through which he wants us to go.

Catherine Marshall

What may seem defeat to us may be victory to him.

C. H. Spurgeon

The difference between winning and losing is how we choose to react to disappointment.

Barbara Johnson

A Father-Son Prayer

Dear Lord, there's no problem that is too big for You. Thank You, Father, for protecting us today, and forever. Amen

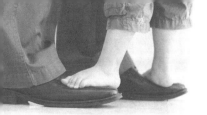

Keeping a Thankful Attitude

And whatever you do, in word or in deed, do everything in the name of the Lord Jesus, giving thanks to God the Father through Him.

Colossians 3:17 HCSB

D o you have a thankful attitude? Hopefully so! After all, you've got plenty of things to be thankful for. Even during those times when you're angry or tired, you're a very lucky person.

Who has given you all the blessings you enjoy? Your parents are responsible, of course. But all of your blessings really start with God. That's why you should say "Thank You" to God many times each day. He's given you so much . . . so thank Him, starting now.

A Timely Tip for Boys

Want to cheer yourself up? Count your blessings. If you need a little cheering up, start counting your blessings . . . and keep counting until you feel better.

More from God's Word

Give thanks to the Lord, for He is good; His faithful love endures forever.

Psalm 118:29 HCSB

I will give You thanks with all my heart.

Psalm 138:1 HCSB

And whatever you do, in word or in deed, do everything in the name of the Lord Jesus, giving thanks to God the Father through Him.

Colossians 3:17 HCSB

A Timely Tip for Dads

Today, as you hug your child or kiss your wife—or as you gaze upon a passing cloud or marvel at a glorious sunset—think of what God has done for you and yours. And, every time you notice a gift from the Giver of all things good, praise Him. His works are marvelous, His gifts are beyond understanding, and His love endures forever.

Some Very Bright Ideas

It is only with gratitude that life becomes rich.

Dietrich Bonhoeffer

It is always possible to be thankful for what is given rather than to complain about what is not given. One or the other becomes a habit of life.

Elisabeth Elliot

When it comes to life, the critical thing is whether you take things for granted or take them with gratitude.

G. K. Chesterton

A Father-Son Prayer

Lord, we will worship You every day. Help us discover the peace that can be ours when we welcome You into our hearts. Amen

Draw a Picture Together about What You Are Thankful For

Encourage Each Other

So encourage each other and give each other strength, just as you are doing now.

1 Thessalonians 5:11 NCV

When other people are sad, what can we do? We can do our best to cheer them up by showing kindness and love.

The Bible tells us that we must care for each other, and when everybody is happy, that's an easy thing to do. But, when people are sad, for whatever reason, it's up to us to speak a kind word or to offer a helping hand.

Do you know someone who is discouraged or sad? If so, perhaps it's time to take matters into your own hands. Think of something you can do to cheer that person up . . . and then do it! You'll make two people happy.

A Timely Tip for Boys

You can't lift other people up without lifting yourself up, too.

More from God's Word

I want their hearts to be encouraged and joined together in love, so that they may have all the riches of assured understanding, and have the knowledge of God's mystery—Christ.

Colossians 2:2 HCSB

And let us be concerned about one another in order to promote love and good works.

Hebrews 10:24 HCSB

Carry one another's burdens; in this way you will fulfill the law of Christ.

Galatians 6:2 HCSB

A Timely Tip for Dads

Be a booster, not a cynic. Cynicism is contagious, and so is optimism. Think and act accordingly.

Some Very Bright Ideas

How many people stop because so few say, "Go!"

Charles Swindoll

Encouragement is the oxygen of the soul.

John Maxwell

My special friends, who know me so well and love me anyway, give me daily encouragement to keep on.

Emilie Barnes

A Father-Son Prayer

Dear Lord, we want to make our family and friends feel better. Please let us say the right words and do the right things now and always. Amen

How Would Jesus Behave?

You did not choose Me, but I chose you. I appointed you that you should go out and produce fruit, and that your fruit should remain, so that whatever you ask the Father in My name, He will give you.

John 15:16 HCSB

If you're not certain whether something is right or wrong, ask yourself a simple question: "What would Jesus do if He were here?" The answer to that question will tell you how to behave yourself.

Jesus was perfect, but we are not. Still, we must try as hard as we can to be like Him. When we do, we will love others, just like Christ loves us.

A Timely Tip for Boys

Want to know what Jesus would do? Then learn what Jesus did!

More from God's Word

Then he told them what they could expect for themselves: "Anyone who intends to come with me has to let me lead."

Luke 9:23 MSG

Whoever is not willing to carry the cross and follow me is not worthy of me. Those who try to hold on to their lives will give up true life. Those who give up their lives for me will hold on to true life.

Matthew 10:38-39 NCV

If anyone would come after me, he must deny himself and take up his cross and follow me.

Mark 8:34 NIV

A Timely Tip for Dads

Talk is cheap. Real ministry has legs. When it comes to discipleship, make sure that your family backs up its words with deeds.

Some Very Bright Ideas

Joy comes not from what we have but from what we are.

C. H. Spurgeon

Being a Christian is more than just an instantaneous conversion; it is like a daily process whereby you grow to be more and more like Christ.

Billy Graham

Service is love in overalls!

Anonymous

A Father-Son Prayer

Dear Lord, we thank You for Your Son Jesus and for His love. Today, we will share His love with our family and friends. Amen

God Knows Best

However, each one must live his life in the situation the Lord assigned when God called him.

1 Corinthians 7:17 HCSB

Here are three things to think about tonight: 1. God loves you. 2. God wants what's best for you. 3. God has a plan for you.

God's plan may not always happen exactly like you want, but remember: God always knows best. Sometimes, even though you may want something very badly, you must still be patient and wait for the right time to get it. And the right time, of course, is determined by God.

Even if you don't get exactly what you want today, you can be sure that God wants what's best for you . . . today, tomorrow, and forever.

A Timely Tip for Boys

God has a plan for the world and for you. When you discover His plan for your life—and when you follow in the footsteps of His Son—you will be rewarded. The place where God is leading you is the place where you must go.

More from God's Word

The Lord says, "I will guide you along the best pathway for your life. I will advise you and watch over you."

Psalm 32:8 NLT

"I say this because I know what I am planning for you," says the Lord. "I have good plans for you, not plans to hurt you. I will give you hope and a good future."

Jeremiah 29:11 NCV

People may make plans in their minds, but the Lord decides what they will do.

Proverbs 16:9 NCV

A Timely Tip for Dads

God has a wonderful plan for your life. And the time to start looking for that plan—and living it—is now. Discovering God's plan begins with prayer, but it doesn't end there. You've also got to work at it.

Some Very Bright Ideas

God must do everything for us. Our part is to yield and trust.

A. W. Tozer

God will never lead you where His strength cannot keep you.

Barbara Johnson

My policy has always been to ask God to help me set goals because I believe God has a plan for every person.

Bill Bright

A Father-Son Prayer

Dear Lord, You have wonderful plans for us. Let us discover those plans so that we can become the people You want us to become. Amen

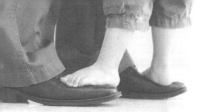

Stop Fighting

It's a mark of good character to avert quarrels, but fools love to pick fights.

Proverbs 20:3 MSG

Since the days of Cain and Abel, people have discovered plenty of things to fight about (Cain and Abel, by the way, were the sons of Adam and Eve). It seems that fighting is a favorite activity for many people, even though it's almost always the wrong thing to do.

Kids should do their best to avoid fights, period. So do yourself a favor: try to avoid senseless scuffles, foolish fights, alarming arguments, and constant conflicts. You'll be glad you did . . . and so will God.

A Timely Tip for Boys

Tempted to fight? Walk away. The best fights are those that never happen.

More from God's Word

A kind man benefits himself, but a cruel man brings disaster on himself.

Proverbs 11:17 HCSB

Love is patient; love is kind.

1 Corinthians 13:4 HCSB

Therefore, God's chosen ones, holy and loved, put on heartfelt compassion, kindness, humility, gentleness, and patience.

Colossians 3:12 HCSB

A Timely Tip for Dads

When it comes to family discussions, parents set the tone. So make sure that your communications are polite and peaceful, not pugnacious or impertinent.

Some Very Bright Ideas

Whatever you do when conflicts arise, be wise. Fight against jumping to quick conclusions and seeing only your side. There are always two sides on the streets of conflict. Look both ways.

Charles Swindoll

When you "win" an argument, what have you really won? Not much!

Criswell Freeman

Some fights are lost even though we win. A bulldog can whip a skunk, but it just isn't worth it.

Vance Havner

A Father-Son Prayer

Dear Lord, when we are tempted to say things or do things that are unkind, help us stay calm and be kind. Amen

Pay Attention to Your Bible

All Scripture is inspired by God and is profitable for teaching, for rebuking, for correcting, for training in righteousness, so that the man of God may be complete, equipped for every good work.

2 Timothy 3:16-17 HCSB

Do you think about the Bible a lot . . . or not? Hopefully, you pay careful attention to the things you learn from God's Word! After all, the Bible is God's message to you. It's not just a book, it's a priceless, one-of-a-kind treasure . . . and it has amazing things to teach you. So start learning about the Bible now, and keep learning about it for as long as you live!

A Timely Tip for Boys

Who's supposed to be taking care of your Bible? If it's you, then take very good care of it; it's by far the most important book you own!

More from God's Word

Man shall not live by bread alone, but by every word that proceeds from the mouth of God.

Matthew 4:4 NKJV

For I am not ashamed of the gospel, because it is God's power for salvation to everyone who believes.

Romans 1:16 HCSB

For the word of God is living and effective and sharper than any two-edged sword, penetrating as far as to divide soul, spirit, joints, and marrow; it is a judge of the ideas and thoughts of the heart.

Hebrews 4:12 HCSB

A Timely Tip for Dads

Our children will learn about Jesus at church and, in some cases, at school. But, the ultimate responsibility for religious teachings should never be delegated to institutions outside the home. As parents, we must teach our children about the love and grace of Jesus Christ by our words and by our actions.

Some Very Bright Ideas

Only through routine, regular exposure to God's Word can you and I draw out the nutrition needed to grow a heart of faith.

Elizabeth George

Nobody ever outgrows Scripture; the book widens and deepens with our years.

C. H. Spurgeon

The more you use your Bible, the more God will use you.

Criswell Freeman

A Father-Son Prayer

Dear Lord, we thank You for the gift of Your Holy Word. We will study Your Bible and trust Your promises today and every day. Amen

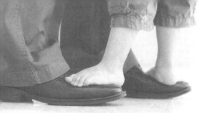

Developing New Habits

For every tree is known by its own fruit.

Luke 6:44 NKJV

Perhaps you've tried to become a more patient person, but you're still falling back into your old habits. If so, don't get discouraged. Instead, become even more determined to become the person God wants you to be.

If you trust God, and if you keep asking Him to help you change bad habits, He will help you make yourself into a new person. So, if at first you don't succeed, keep praying. If you keep asking, you'll eventually get the answers you need.

A Timely Tip for Boys

Choose your habits carefully: habits are easier to make than they are to break, so be careful!

More from God's Word

Dear friend, I pray that you may prosper in every way and be in good health, just as your soul prospers.

3 John 1:2 HCSB

Therefore, brothers, by the mercies of God, I urge you to present your bodies as a living sacrifice, holy and pleasing to God; this is your spiritual worship.

Romans 12:1 HCSB

Don't you know that you are God's sanctuary and that the Spirit of God lives in you?

1 Corinthians 3:16 HCSB

A Timely Tip for Dads

First you make your habits; then your habits make you. So it's always a good time to think about the kind of person your habits are making you.

Some Very Bright Ideas

If you want to form a new habit, get to work. If you want to break a bad habit, get on your knees.

Marie T. Freeman

You can build up a set of good habits so that you habitually take the Christian way without thought.

E. Stanley Jones

Just as iron, even without willing it, is drawn by a magnet, so is a slave to bad habits dragged about by them.

John Climacus

A Father-Son Prayer

Dear Lord, today, we're asking for Your help. Please help us do things that are pleasing to You, and help us form habits that are pleasing to You. Amen

The Boy in the Mirror

For you made us only a little lower than God, and you crowned us with glory and honor.

Psalm 8:5 NLT

D o you really like the person you see when you look into the mirror? You should! After all, the person in the mirror is a very special person who is made—and loved—by God.

In fact, you are loved in many, many ways: God loves you, your parents love you, and your family loves you, for starters. So you should love yourself, too.

So here's something to think about: since God thinks you're special, and since so many people think you're special, isn't it about time for you to agree with them? Of course it is! It's time to say, "You're very wonderful and very special," to the person you see in the mirror.

A Timely Tip for Boys

God loves you . . . and you should, too.

More from God's Word

God began doing a good work in you, and I am sure he will continue it until it is finished when Jesus Christ comes again.

Philippians 1:6 NCV

For You formed my inward parts; You covered me in my mother's womb. I will praise You, for I am fearfully and wonderfully made; Marvelous are Your works.

Psalm 139:13-14 NKJV

You're blessed when you're content with just who you are— no more, no less. That's the moment you find yourselves proud owners of everything that can't be bought.

Matthew 5:5 MSG

A Timely Tip for Dads

Your family's collective self-esteem starts at the head of the household and works its way down from there. It's not enough to concern yourself with your child's self-image; you should also strive to become comfortable with your own self-image, too.

Some Very Bright Ideas

A healthy self-identity is seeing yourself as God sees you—
no more and no less.

Josh McDowell

To like ourselves does not mean we are full of pride—it
simply means we accept ourselves as God's creation.

Joyce Meyer

If you can forgive the person you were, accept the person
you are, and believe in the person you will become, you are
headed for joy. So celebrate your life.

Barbara Johnson

A Father-Son Prayer

*Dear Lord, thank You for Your Son. Because Jesus loves us, we
know that we are protected. Because Jesus loves us, we know
that we have value. Because Jesus loves us, we know that our
future is secure. Amen*

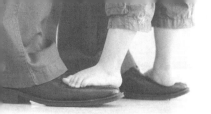

It's Not Hard to Be Kind

Therefore, God's chosen ones, holy and loved, put on heartfelt compassion, kindness, humility, gentleness, and patience.

Colossians 3:12 HCSB

How hard is it to say a kind word? Not very! Yet sometimes we're so busy that we forget to say the very things that might make other people feel better.

We should always try to say nice things to our families and friends. And when we feel like saying something that's not so nice, perhaps we should stop and think before we say it. Kind words help; cruel words hurt. It's as simple as that. And, when we say the right thing at the right time, we give a gift that can change someone's day or someone's life.

A Timely Tip for Boys

It's good to tell your family how you feel about them, but that's not enough. You should also show them how you feel with good deeds.

More from God's Word

Just as you want others to do for you, do the same for them.

Luke 6:31 HCSB

Finally, all of you be of one mind, having compassion for one another; love as brothers, be tenderhearted, be courteous.

1 Peter 3:8 NKJV

Love is patient; love is kind.

1 Corinthians 13:4 HCSB

A Timely Tip for Dads

Wise dads understand that kindness matters, and, for that matter, it matters a lot.

Some Very Bright Ideas

When you launch an act of kindness out into the crosswinds of life, it will blow kindness back to you.

Dennis Swanberg

He who sows courtesy reaps friendship, and he who plants kindness gathers love.

St. Basil the Great

Sometimes one little spark of kindness is all it takes to reignite the light of hope in a heart that's blinded by pain.

Barbara Johnson

A Father-Son Prayer

Dear Lord, it's always the right time to be kind. Help us be kind today, tomorrow, and every day of our lives. Amen

Obey God and Be Happy

I will praise you, Lord, with all my heart. I will tell all the miracles you have done. I will be happy because of you; God Most High, I will sing praises to your name.

Psalm 9:1-2 NCV

Do you want to be happy? Here are some things you should do: Love God and His Son, Jesus; obey the Golden Rule; and always try to do the right thing. When you do these things, you'll discover that happiness goes hand-in-hand with good behavior.

The happiest people do not misbehave; the happiest people are not cruel or greedy. The happiest people don't say unkind things. The happiest people are those who love God and follow His rules—starting with the Golden one.

A Timely Tip for Boys

Even if you're a very good person, you shouldn't expect to be happy all the time. Sometimes, things will happen to make you sad, and it's okay to be sad when bad things happen to you or to your friends and family. But remember: through good times and bad, you'll always be happier if you obey the rules of your Father in heaven. So obey them!

More from God's Word

How happy are those whose way is blameless, who live according to the law of the Lord! Happy are those who keep His decrees and seek Him with all their heart.

Psalm 119:1-2 HCSB

Happy is the one whose help is the God of Jacob, whose hope is in the Lord his God.

Psalm 146:5 HCSB

How happy is everyone who fears the Lord, who walks in His ways!

Psalm 128:1 HCSB

A Timely Tip for Dads

Do you want to make your home life a continual feast? Learn to laugh and love, but not necessarily in that order.

Some Very Bright Ideas

Smile—it increases your face value.

Anonymous

True happiness consists only in the enjoyment of God. His favor is life, and his loving-kindness is better than life.

Arthur W. Pink

We will never be happy until we make God the source of our fulfillment and the answer to our longings.

Stormie Omartian

A Father-Son Prayer

Dear Lord, we have more blessings than we can count. Today and every day, we will be happy Christians as we give thanks for Your gifts and for Your Son. Amen

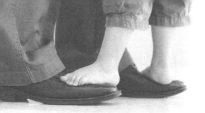

Living by God's Rules

Does the LORD delight in burnt offerings and sacrifices as much as in obeying the voice of the LORD? To obey is better than sacrifice….

1 Samuel 15:22 NIV

God has rules, and He wants you to obey them. He wants you to be fair, honest, and kind. He wants you to behave yourself, and He wants you to respect your parents. God has other rules, too, and you'll find them in a very special book: the Bible.

With a little help from your parents, you can figure out God's rules. And then, it's up to you to live by them. When you do, everybody will be pleased—you will be pleased, your parents will be pleased . . . and God will be pleased, too.

A Timely Tip for Boys

When you obey God, you'll feel better about yourself. When you don't obey Him, you'll feel worse.

More from God's Word

The world and its desires pass away, but the man who does the will of God lives forever.

1 John 2:17 NIV

So roll up your sleeves, put your mind in gear, be totally ready to receive the gift that's coming when Jesus arrives. Don't lazily slip back into those old grooves of evil, doing just what you feel like doing. You didn't know any better then; you do now. As obedient children, let yourselves be pulled into a way of life shaped by God's life, a life energetic and blazing with holiness.

1 Peter 1:13-15 MSG

Here is my final advice: Honor God and obey his commands.

Ecclesiastes 12:13 ICB

A Timely Tip for Dads

Your children will learn about life from many sources; the most important source should be you. So remember that the lectures you give are never as important as the ones you live.

Some Very Bright Ideas

Only he who believes is obedient. Only he who is obedient believes.

Dietrich Bonhoeffer

Obey God one step at a time, then the next step will come into view.

Catherine Marshall

Obedience to God is our job. The results of that obedience are God's.

Elisabeth Elliot

A Father-Son Prayer

Dear Lord, the Bible teaches us to follow Jesus, and that's what we want to do. So, Father, please help us show other people what it means to be good people and good Christians. Amen

Draw a Picture Together about Being Happy

Patience and the Golden Rule

Always be humble and gentle. Be patient and accept each other with love.

Ephesians 4:2 ICB

Jesus gave us a Golden Rule for living: He said that we should treat other people in the same way that we want to be treated. And because we want other people to be patient with us, we, in turn, must be patient with them.

Being patient with other people means treating them with kindness, respect, and understanding. It means waiting our turn when we're standing in line and forgiving our friends when they've done something we don't like. Sometimes, it's hard to be patient, but we've got to do our best. And when we do, we're following the Golden Rule—God's rule for how to treat others—and everybody wins!

A Timely Tip for Boys

Patience pays; recklessness doesn't.

More from God's Word

Be completely humble and gentle; be patient, bearing with one another in love.

Ephesians 4:2 NIV

Wherefore seeing we also are compassed about with so great a cloud of witnesses, let us lay aside every weight, and the sin which doth so easily beset us, and let us run with patience the race that is set before us....

Hebrews 12:1 KJV

Yet the LORD longs to be gracious to you; he rises to show you compassion. For the LORD is a God of justice. Blessed are all who wait for him!

Isaiah 30:18 NIV

A Timely Tip for Dads

Be patient. Children are supposed to be more impulsive than adults; after all, they're still kids. So be understanding of your child's limitations and understanding of his imperfections.

Some Very Bright Ideas

If only we could be as patient with other people as God is with us!

Jim Gallery

God is more patient with us than we are with ourselves.

Max Lucado

God never gives up on you, so don't you ever give up on Him.

Marie T. Freeman

A Father-Son Prayer

Dear Lord, help us learn to be patient, kind, courteous, and cooperative with our family and with our friends. Amen

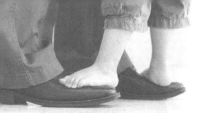

Listen to Your Parents

Listen carefully to wisdom; set your mind on understanding.

Proverbs 2:2 NCV

Are you the kind of boy who listens carefully to the things your parents tell you? You should. Your parents want the very best for you. They want you to be happy and healthy; they want you to be smart and to do smart things. Your parents have much to teach you, and you have much to learn. So listen carefully to the things your mom and dad have to say. And ask lots of questions. When you do, you'll soon discover that your parents have lots of answers . . . lots of very good answers.

A Timely Tip for Boys

Your parents love you and want to help you. Their job is to help . . . your job is to listen carefully to the things they say.

More from God's Word

Honor your father and your mother so that you may have a long life in the land that the Lord your God is giving you.

Exodus 20:12 HCSB

Listen, my son, to your father's instruction and do not forsake your mother's teaching.

Proverbs 1:8 NIV

Let them first learn to do their duty to their own family and to repay their parents or grandparents. That pleases God.

1 Timothy 5:4 NCV

A Timely Tip for Dads

For most parents, the temptation to lecture is great; it takes conscious effort to hold one's tongue until one's ears are fully engaged. When a parent is able to do so, his or her efforts are usually rewarded.

Some Very Bright Ideas

Listening is loving.

Zig Ziglar

The cliché is true: People don't care what we know until they know we care.

Rick Warren

The first duty of love is to listen.

Paul Tillich

One of the best ways to encourage someone who's hurting is with your ears—by listening.

Barbara Johnson

A Father-Son Prayer

Dear Lord, let us learn as much as we can as soon as we can, and let us be good examples for other people to follow. Amen

Be Hopeful

We have this hope—like a sure and firm anchor of the soul—that enters the inner sanctuary behind the curtain.

Hebrews 6:19 HCSB

Are you a hope-filled boy? Hopefully so!

When you stop to think about it, you have lots of reasons to be hopeful: God loves you, your family loves you, and you've got a very bright future ahead of you. So trust God, and be hopeful. When you do, you'll be a happier person . . . and God will smile.

A Timely Tip for Boys

As long as God is in His heaven, there's always hope . . . so don't give up!

More from God's Word

Let us hold on to the confession of our hope without wavering, for He who promised is faithful.

Hebrews 10:23 HCSB

Hope deferred makes the heart sick.

Proverbs 13:12 NKJV

Sustain me as You promised, and I will live; do not let me be ashamed of my hope.

Psalm 119:116 HCSB

A Timely Tip for Dads

Worried about your family or your future? Since God has promised to guide and protect you—now and forever—you should never lose hope.

Some Very Bright Ideas

Many things are possible for the person who has hope. Even more is possible for the person who has faith. And still more is possible for the person who knows how to love. But everything is possible for the person who practices all three virtues.

Brother Lawrence

Life with Christ is an endless hope, without him a hopeless end.

Anonymous

Our hope in Christ for the future is the mainstream of our joy.

C. H. Spurgeon

A Father-Son Prayer

Dear God, help us remember to keep hope in our hearts . . . and praise on our lips for You! Amen

Time with God

Careful planning puts you ahead in the long run; hurry and scurry puts you further behind.

Proverbs 21:5 MSG

How much time do you spend getting to know God? A lot? A little? Almost none? Hopefully, you answered, "a lot."

God loved this world so much that He sent His Son to save it. And now only one real question remains for you: what will you do in response to God's love? God deserves your prayers, your obedience, and your love—and He deserves these things all day every day, not just on Sunday mornings.

A Timely Tip for Boys

You should plan to spend some time with God every day . . . and you should stick to your plan!

More from God's Word

You can't go wrong when you love others. When you add up everything in the law code, the sum total is love. But make sure that you don't get so absorbed and exhausted in taking care of all your day-by-day obligations that you lose track of the time and doze off, oblivious to God.

Romans 13:10-11 MSG

Jesus said, "You're tied down to the mundane; I'm in touch with what is beyond your horizons. You live in terms of what you see and touch. I'm living on other terms. I told you that you were missing God in all this. You're at a dead end. If you won't believe I am who I say I am, you're at the dead end of sins. You're missing God in your lives."

John 8:23-24 MSG

A Timely Tip for Dads

Do first things first, and keep your focus on high-priority tasks. And remember this: your highest priority should be your relationship with God and His Son.

Some Very Bright Ideas

We often become mentally and spiritually worn out because we're so busy.

Franklin Graham

Frustration is not the will of God. There is time to do anything and everything that God wants us to do.

Elisabeth Elliot

Getting things accomplished isn't nearly as important as taking time for love.

Janette Oke

A Father-Son Prayer

Dear Lord, we have lots to do every day, but nothing we do is more important than spending time with You. Help us remember to pray often and to read Your Bible every day. Amen

You Don't Have to Be Perfect

You're blessed when you're content with just who you are—no more, no less. That's the moment you find yourselves proud owners of everything that can't be bought.

Matthew 5:5 MSG

When God made you, He gave you special talents and opportunities that are yours and yours alone. That means you're a very special, one-of-a-kind person, but that doesn't mean that you should expect to be perfect. After all, only one earthly being ever lived life to perfection, and He was, of course, Jesus. And Jesus loves you even when you're not perfect. Your parents feel the same way. And if all those people love you, you should love yourself, too.

A Timely Tip for Boys

The world isn't perfect; your family and friends aren't perfect; and you aren't perfect—and that's okay: We'll all have plenty of time to be perfect in heaven. Until then, we should all be compassionate, forgiving Christians.

More from God's Word

But God, who is abundant in mercy, because of His great love that He had for us, made us alive with the Messiah even though we were dead in trespasses. By grace you are saved!

Ephesians 2:4-5 HCSB

Do you not know that friendship with the world is hostility toward God? So whoever wants to be the world's friend becomes God's enemy.

James 4:4 HCSB

Do not be conformed to this age, but be transformed by the renewing of your mind, so that you may discern what is the good, pleasing, and perfect will of God.

Romans 12:2 HCSB

A Timely Tip for Dads

You know that your kids can't be perfect all the time. . . and it's up to you to make sure that they know they're not expected to be perfect all the time.

Some Very Bright Ideas

The happiest people in the world are not those who have no problems, but the people who have learned to live with those things that are less than perfect.

James Dobson

Bear with the faults of others as you would have them bear with yours.

Phillips Brooks

Better to do something imperfectly than to do nothing perfectly.

Robert Schuller

A Father-Son Prayer

Dear Lord, we're certainly not perfect, but You love us anyway. Thank You for Your love and for Your Son. Amen

Thinking about Your Thoughts

Set your minds on what is above, not on what is on the earth.

Colossians 3:2 HCSB

Do you try to think about things that are honorable, true, and pleasing to God? The Bible says that you should. Do you lift your hopes and your prayers to God many times each day? The Bible says that you should. Do you turn away from bad thoughts and bad people? The Bible says that you should.

The Bible instructs you to guard your thoughts against things that are hurtful or wrong. And when you turn away from the bad and turn instead toward God and His Son Jesus, you will be protected and you will be blessed.

A Timely Tip for Boys

Good thoughts create good deeds. Good thoughts lead to good deeds and bad thoughts lead elsewhere. So guard your thoughts accordingly.

More from God's Word

So prepare your minds for service and have self-control.

1 Peter 1:13 NCV

Those who are pure in their thinking are happy, because they will be with God.

Matthew 5:8 NCV

And now, dear brothers and sisters, let me say one more thing as I close this letter. Fix your thoughts on what is true and honorable and right. Think about things that are pure and lovely and admirable. Think about things that are excellent and worthy of praise.

Philippians 4:8 NLT

A Timely Tip for Dads

Guard your own thoughts. Most children are incredibly in-tuitive. Your child may be far more attuned to your thoughts than you realize. So guard your thoughts—and your emotions—accordingly.

Some Very Bright Ideas

God's cure for evil thinking is to fill our minds with that which is good.

George Sweeting

It is the thoughts and intents of the heart that shape a person's life.

John Eldredge

Make yourselves nests of pleasant thoughts.

John Ruskin

A Father-Son Prayer

Dear Lord, help us think good thoughts—and help us do good things—now and always. Amen

Choices Matter

The thing you should want most is God's kingdom and doing what God wants. Then all these other things you need will be given to you.

Matthew 6:33 NCV

There's really no way to get around it: choices matter. If you make good choices, good things will usually happen to you. And if you make bad choices, bad things will usually happen.

The next time you have an important choice to make, ask yourself this: "Am I doing what God wants me to do?" If you can answer that question with a great big "YES," then go ahead. But if you're not sure if the choice you are about to make is right, slow down. Why? Because choices matter . . . a lot!

A Timely Tip for Boys

First you make choices . . . and pretty soon those choices begin to shape your life. That's why you must make smart choices or face the consequences of making dumb ones.

More from God's Word

Who is wise and understanding among you? He should show his works by good conduct with wisdom's gentleness.

James 3:13 HCSB

Even a young man is known by his actions—by whether his behavior is pure and upright.

Proverbs 20:11 HCSB

Lead a tranquil and quiet life in all godliness and dignity.

1 Timothy 2:2 HCSB

A Timely Tip for Dads

Some matters should be strictly up to you, the parent. These kinds of choices include issues of personal health and safety and the core principles by which you, as a concerned dad, intend to raise your family.

Some Very Bright Ideas

No matter how many books you read, no matter how many schools you attend, you're never really wise until you start making wise choices.

Marie T. Freeman

The power of choosing good or evil is within the reach of all.

Origen of Alexandria

Life is a series of choices between the bad, the good, and the best. Everything depends on how we choose.

Vance Havner

A Father-Son Prayer

Dear Lord, there are so many choices for us to make, and we want to choose wisely. So, we will read the Bible and follow Your teachings tonight, tomorrow, and forever. Amen

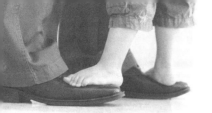

Pleasing God Is More Important Than Pleasing Friends

For am I now trying to win the favor of people, or God? Or am I striving to please people? If I were still trying to please people, I would not be a slave of Christ.

Galatians 1:10 HCSB

A re you a people-pleaser or a God-pleaser? Hopefully, you're far more concerned with pleasing God than you are with pleasing your friends. But face facts: even if you're a devoted Christian, you're still going to feel the urge to impress your friends—and sometimes that urge will be strong.

Here's your choice: you can choose to please God first, or you can fall victim to peer pressure. The choice is yours—and so are the consequences.

A Timely Tip for Boys

Make up your mind to find friends who will help you become a better person.

More from God's Word

Do not be misled: "Bad company corrupts good character."

1 Corinthians 15:33 NIV

Don't become partners with those who reject God. How can you make a partnership out of right and wrong? That's not partnership; that's war. Is light best friends with dark?

2 Corinthians 6:14 MSG

Friend, don't go along with evil. Model the good. The person who does good does God's work. The person who does evil falsifies God, doesn't know the first thing about God.

3 John 1:11 MSG

A Timely Tip for Dads

Put peer pressure to work for you: How? By associating with men who, by their actions and their words, will encourage you to become a better person.

Some Very Bright Ideas

You can't run with the bad boys and walk like a good man.

Bill Dye

It wasn't the apple, it was the pair.

Anonymous

It is impossible to please everybody. It's not impossible to please God. So try pleasing God.

Criswell Freeman

A Father-Son Prayer

Dear Lord, the Bible teaches us that pleasing people is not nearly as important as pleasing You. Let us please You, Lord, today and always. Amen

Be a Good Samaritan

Never walk away from someone who deserves help; your hand is God's hand for that person.

Proverbs 3:27 MSG

Sometimes we would like to help make the world a better place, but we're not sure how to do it. Jesus told the story of the "Good Samaritan," a man who helped a fellow traveler when no one else would. We, too, should be good Samaritans when we find people who need our help. A good place to start helping other people is at home. And of course, we should also offer our help at school and at church.

Another way that we can help other people is to pray for them. God always hears our prayers, so we should talk with Him as often as we can. When we do, we're not only doing a wonderful thing for the people we pray for, we're also doing a wonderful thing for ourselves, too. Why? Because we feel better about ourselves when we're helping other people. And the more we help others, the better we should feel about ourselves.

A Timely Tip for Boys

Martin Luther wrote, "Faith never asks whether good works are to be done, but has done them before there is time to ask the question, and it is always doing them." So when in doubt, do something good!

More from God's Word

When we have the opportunity to help anyone, we should do it. But we should give special attention to those who are in the family of believers.

Galatians 6:10 NCV

You address me as "Teacher" and "Master," and rightly so. That is what I am. So if I, the Master and Teacher, washed your feet, you must now wash each other's feet. I've laid down a pattern for you. What I've done, you do.

John 13:15 MSG

A Timely Tip for Dads

Preach, teach, and reach . . . out! When it comes to teaching our children about helping others, our sermons are not as important as our service. Charity should start at home—with parents—and work its way down the family tree from there.

Some Very Bright Ideas

Encouraging others means helping people, looking for the best in them, and trying to bring out their positive qualities.

John Maxwell

Make it a rule, and pray to God to help you to keep it, never, if possible, to lie down at night without being able to say: "I have made one human being at least a little wiser, or a little happier, or at least a little better this day."

Charles Kingsley

Do all the good you can. By all the means you can. In all the ways you can. In all the places you can. At all the times you can. To all the people you can. As long as ever you can.

John Wesley

A Father-Son Prayer

Dear Lord, Your Son Jesus was never selfish. Let us follow in His footsteps by sharing with those who need our help. Amen

Look Before You Leap

Enthusiasm without knowledge is not good. If you act too quickly, you might make a mistake.

Proverbs 19:2 NCV

Are you sometimes just a little bit impulsive? Do you sometimes fail to look before you leap? If so, God wants you to be a little bit more careful—or maybe a lot more careful!

The Bible makes it clear: we're supposed to behave wisely, not carelessly. But sometimes we're tempted to rush ahead and do things before we think about them.

So do yourself a big favor—slow down, think things through, and look carefully before you leap.

A Timely Tip for Boys

No so fast! If you're about to do something, but you're not sure if it's the right thing to do, slow down! It's better to make a good decision than a fast decision.

More from God's Word

The wise inherit honor, but fools are put to shame!

Proverbs 3:35 NLT

Grow a wise heart—you'll do yourself a favor; keep a clear head—you'll find a good life.

Proverbs 19:8 MSG

The one who walks with the wise will become wise, but a companion of fools will suffer harm.

Proverbs 13:20 HCSB

A Timely Tip for Dads

It's always a good time to put the brakes on impulsive behavior . . . theirs and yours!

Some Very Bright Ideas

If you don't look before you leap, you may start having regrets even before you land.

Criswell Freeman

Wisdom always waits for the right time to act, while emotion always pushes for action right now.

Joyce Meyer

Sometimes, being wise is nothing more than slowing down long enough to think about things before you do them.

Criswell Freeman

A Father-Son Prayer

Dear Lord, sometimes we're in a hurry. Today, help us slow down and think about the things we're about to do before we do them, not after. Amen

God's Greatest Promise

I assure you: Anyone who believes has eternal life.

John 6:47 HCSB

It's time to remind yourself of a promise that God made a long time ago—the promise that God sent His Son Jesus to save the world and to save you! And when you stop to think about it, there can be no greater promise than that.

No matter where you are, God is with you. God loves you, and He sent His Son so that you can live forever in heaven with your loved ones. WOW! That's the greatest promise in the history of the universe. The end.

A Timely Tip for Boys

God's gift of eternal life is amazing. Talk to your dad about God's promise of eternal life, and what that promise means to you.

More from God's Word

I have written these things to you who believe in the name of the Son of God, so that you may know that you have eternal life.

1 John 5:13 HCSB

We do not want you to be uninformed, brothers, concerning those who are asleep, so that you will not grieve like the rest, who have no hope. Since we believe that Jesus died and rose again, in the same way God will bring with Him those who have fallen asleep through Jesus.

1 Thessalonians 4:13-14 HCSB

Jesus said to her, "I am the resurrection and the life. The one who believes in Me, even if he dies, will live. Everyone who lives and believes in Me will never die—ever. Do you believe this?"

John 11:25-26 HCSB

A Timely Tip for Dads

God has created heaven and given you a way to get there. The rest is up to you. Make sure your children know the way.

Some Very Bright Ideas

The gift of God is eternal life, spiritual life, abundant life through faith in Jesus Christ, the Living Word of God.

Anne Graham Lotz

And because we know Christ is alive, we have hope for the present and hope for life beyond the grave.

Billy Graham

Teach us to set our hopes on heaven, to hold firmly to the promise of eternal life, so that we can withstand the struggles and storms of this world.

Max Lucado

A Father-Son Prayer

Dear Lord, Jesus died so that we can live forever with Him in heaven. Thank You, Father, for Your Son and for the priceless gift of eternal life. Amen

Jesus:
the proof of God's love.

–

Philip Yancey

Draw a Picture of You and Your Dad Playing a Game